2

# Language Links

JIM SWEETMAN

CollinsEducational
*An imprint of* HarperCollins*Publishers*

# 2
# Language Links

JIM SWEETMAN

CollinsEducational
*An imprint of* HarperCollins*Publishers*

ISBN 0 00 323024 4



First published by CollinsEducational,
*an imprint of* HarperCollins*Publishers*
77–85 Fulham Palace Road, London W6 8JB.

Cover and text designed by Christie Archer
Cover illustration by Simon Fell
Edited by Stephen Attmore

Typeset by CG Graphic Services, Aylesbury

Printed and bound in Hong Kong

# Contents

# Acknowledgements

The following authors and publishers are thanked for permission to reproduce their material: p10 Stephen Rabley, *Media Crew 1: GOOD NEWS BAD NEWS*, Armada, an imprint of HarperCollins *Publishers* Limited; article about stereo systems from *Which?* February 1992, published by Consumers' Association, London; p11 untitled poem by Ken Norris; 'Customs & Excise Leaflet 700/1/91: Should I be Registered for VAT?' Crown copyright, reproduced with permission of the Controller of Her Majesty's Stationery Office; p14 copyright © 1984 by Judith Newman. Reprinted by permission of Scholastic Canada Ltd, 123 Newkirk Road, Richmond Hill, Ontario, Canada L4C 3G5; p16 *The Diary of Samuel Pepys: A New and Complete Transcription* edited by Robert Latham and William Matthews © Bell & Hyman Limited 1974. Reprinted by permission of HarperCollins *Publishers* Limited; p17 *Just 17* for the 'We've just split up and can't cope' letter; letter by F Klaptocz, Twickenham from *Which?* February 1992, published by the Consumers' Association, London; Richard A Cater of Ipswich for his letter to *Daily Mail;* p23 Cornhill Insurance for the Motor Vehicle Theft Report form; p28 spreads from *Frosty* written by Ginny Lapage and illustrated by Caroline Sharpe, published by Collins Educational, an imprint of HarperCollins *Publishers* Limited; p29 'Ban on trade in leopard skins may be lifted' article by Polly Ghazi from *The Observer*, 2 Feb 1992; p36 AA Publishing for spread from *Where To Go In The Countryside;* Collins Educational, an imprint of HarperCollins *Publishers,* for page from *Business Studies for GCSE* by Renée Huggett; *The Observer Magazine* for part of 'The Busted' article; p38 extract from *MIZZ* issue 84 courtesy of Holborn Publishing Group; p39 extract from *The Outdoor Traveler's Guide: Caribbean* Text © Kay Showker, published by Stewart, Tabori & Chang Inc, New York; p40 reproduced from *An Usborne Introduction to Keyboards and Computer Music* by permission of Usborne Publishing Ltd, London; 'Scot free?' article © The Guardian; p41 The Bedfordshire and Cambridgeshire Wildlife Trust; page taken from *The Kingfisher Book of Electronics.* Published by Kingfisher Books. Copyright © Grisewood and Dempsey Ltd 1984; p42 spread from *First Impressions* published by Collins Educational, an imprint of HarperCollins *Publishers;* p48 Environmental Investigation Agency for leaflet; 'Taxing times' diagram © The Guardian; *The Observer Magazine* for 'Consumer Guide'; p57 © Times Supplements Ltd 1988 extracts from article 'Trials and Tribulations of an ''independent'' life' by Linda Blackbourne and Nicholas Pyke, TES 16.12.88; p58 (top) *The Independent Magazine;* (lower) © Times Supplements Ltd; pp60-1 IFAW for 'I'm against hunting…and I vote'; Amnesty International for their leaflet; Crisis, 7 Whitechapel Road, London E1 1DU and Lowe, Howard, Spink for their leaflet; Wood Green Animal Shelter for permission to reproduce the National Pet Register leaflet; Department of Health's 1986 Anti-Drugs Campaign, Crown copyright, reproduced with the permission of the Controller of Her Majesty's Stationery Office; extract taken from Mission Aviation Fellowship's 1991 Annual Report (MAF, Ingles Manor, Castle Hill Avenue, Folkestone, Kent CT20 2TN); 'Thank God Someone's Making Waves' leaflet reproduced with the permission of Greenpeace Ltd; part of teacher membership leaflet courtesy of WWF; p67 Thomson Tour Operators Ltd for the front cover and inside page from 'Skytours' brochure; pp69-70 extract from *India File* by Trevor Fishlock courtesy of John Murray (Publishers) Ltd; pp74-6 extract from *Empty World* by John Christopher © the author; p80 'Why can you see yourself in a mirror?' and 'Why does glue stick things together?' taken from *Why Things Are?* published by Kingfisher Books. Copyright © Grisewood and Dempsey Ltd 1983; other 3 extracts from *Notes and Queries* published by Fourth Estate Ltd, © 1991 Guardian Newspapers Ltd; p83 article and artwork logo from *Crocodiles and Alligators* © Weldon Owen Pty Ltd; 'Heart' from *Amazing Origami for Children* by Steve and Megumi Biddle published by Arrow Books; we are grateful to the Scientific Committee on Antarctic Research (SCAR) for permission to reproduce the extract from 'A visitor's introduction to the Antarctic and its environment'; pp84-5 'Root the Loot' game by Jez Alborough, from *The Great Games Book*, A & C Black (Publishers) Limited; pp89-91 'Aunt Kate's Goomer-Dust' taken from *The Devil's Pretty Daughter and Other Ozark Folk Tales,* collected by Vance Randolph, 1955, Columbia University Press, New York. Used by permission of the publisher; pp92-3 extract from *Dances with Wolves* (Penguin Books, 1991) © Michael Blake, 1988; pp94-5 extract from 'The Trap' © Robert Westall 1990, first published by Macmillan Publishers Ltd; p97 Puffin Classics for permission to show the *Black Beauty* and *Watership Down* covers; HarperCollins*Publishers* for the covers of *James and the Giant Peach* and *The Hobbit; Secret Diary of Adrian Mole aged 13¾* illustrated by Caroline Holden, published by Mandarin Paperbacks; pp103-5 front cover and extract from *Stone Alone* by Bill Wyman and Ray Coleman copyright © Ripple Productions Ltd, 1990; p108 Oxfam for 'Tanked up in Taunton' article; Earthscan Publications Ltd for the extract 'Going, Going' from their booklet 'Defending the Future'; p109 Save the Children for extract from 1991 Review and section from 'Children on the move need your help' leaflet; pp118-9 'The Book of the Banshees' review and extract from 'toy industry' article *The Observer;* Dire Straits album review, *Q* magazine; Barry Norman for video review © The Guardian; © Times Supplements Ltd 1992 for 'Air of wit' by Mick Martin, TES 28.2.92 and extract from 'Book List: Curriculum Guides', TES 7.2.92; 'Inspector Morse' article © The Daily Telegraph plc, 1992.

Every effort has been made to contact the holders of copyright material, but if any have been inadvertently overlooked the publishers will be pleased to make the necessary arrangements at the first opportunity. We have not been able to trace the source of the 'tobacco' extract on page 39; any help with this would be appreciated.

**PHOTOGRAPHS**

Bryan & Cherry Alexander 87B; © ALLSPORT/John Gichigi 35T, Gary M Prior 35C; Dee Banks 66, 67B; BAS 72-3C; BBC TV News 23TL; Frank Bird 10, 28, 36, 40-2, 60-1, 67T, 69, 83, 97, 103; Anne Bolt 39; Cambridge Newspapers Ltd 32-3; Cambridge Water Company 120; Colorsport 49; Compix 110B; Mark Edwards/Still Pictures 107, 110T; Richard & Sally Greenhill 9T, 9B, 23CR, 50T, 50C, 63; The Hulton Picture Company 16R; The Frank Lane Picture Agency 72-3B; Nigel Luckhurst 23BR, 50B, 81, 87T, 125T; by courtesy of the National Portrait Gallery, London 16T; NASA 72-3T; Network SouthEast 62; Popperfoto 16L, 104-5, 106, 126B; Elliott Landy/Redferns 68; RMN 126T; Adrian Rowland 35B, 57, 58L, 58R; Swedish Tourist Board 122-5; Syndication International 58T, 126C; John Walmsley 9C, 34, 115CR; ZEFA 70-1

# Introduction

## USING *LANGUAGE LINKS TWO*

The two books in the *Language Links* series present the information which secondary school students are now expected to learn about language and writing as part of what is termed 'knowledge about language'. Both books stress that the clear presentation of information, the close study of examples and the use of language in real, purposeful contexts is the key to success in writing.

*Language Links Two* approaches the development of writing skills by showing students the characteristic features of different types of writing. Writers make meaning through choice – they choose the writing structures and word patterns which most closely allow them to express the meanings they hope to communicate. As they write, they refer back and modify either of these or give their writing other features of their own choosing.

For many writers, these choices are often unconscious, and familiarity with a particular type of writing allows it to be reproduced almost on demand. This familiarity comes with acquaintance and practice over a long period and may well be part of our definition of what makes a successful writer.

Other writers, however, face difficulties in encountering any writing task. Recent research suggests that a major element in writing failure for many writers may concern their failure to recognise exactly what they are being asked to do and their ability to define for themselves what a successful version should be like.

*Language Links Two* approaches those connected problems from two aspects. It sets out, firstly, to help students understand the writing demands that particular writing tasks place upon them and, secondly, it endeavours to equip them with the knowledge and experience to approach such tasks with confidence. This is the principle on which the National Curriculum bases all its approaches to what is termed 'knowledge about language' – the notion that usage and understanding go hand in hand.

*Language Links Two* also recognises that writing development is recursive and that continuing practice and reinforcement lead to an improvement in performance. So does the help of peers in rephrasing, analysing and evaluating what is written. Finally, carefully selected and extensive examples illustrate how context, purpose and audience are vital aspects of the writing process.

Separate self-contained units deal with different aspects of personal, informational, persuasive and narrative writing. Writing types such as eye-witness report, opinion and persuasion, and comparison and analysis, are distinguished by interesting and innovative examples and rehearsed through authentic assignments. For the different writing types explored, there is extensive guidance as to how students can make use of them and modify them for their own purposes.

The examples are drawn from a wide range of non-narrative material and both classic and contemporary fiction. Writing is presented as a cross-disciplinary exercise and many of the extracts are relevant to other subject areas within the National Curriculum and to its cross-curricular themes. The information about writing types is repeated in handy fact boxes for easy reference.

Also included is a specialist section concerned with the kinds of detailed and lengthy writing – projects, theme or topic-based research and field study – which the higher levels of the National Curriculum structure demand in Science, History, Geography and Technology.

*Language Links Two* is designed to stand on its own as a unique and practical guide to writing but it also relates closely to, and offers language support for, pupils working with the Collins English Programme Pupil's Books and Teacher's Resources.

Jim Sweetman

# 1

# Write from the start

## TYPES OF WRITING

When you start to plan a piece of writing, the first things you have to consider are your *purpose* – why you are writing and what you want to say – and your *audience* – who you are writing for. It is quite likely that you will have more than one purpose in mind as you think about and draft your writing and, perhaps, more than one audience.

Often you will be given a purpose for writing in the task you are set. You may be asked to *describe* or *explain*, to *analyse* or *compare*, or to give your *opinion* or say what you know about something. You may also be told to write in a particular form. Letters, playscripts, poems, short paragraphs and even books are all different *forms* of writing. Although you may not have thought hard about this way of looking at writing, you already know something about it from your experiences as a writer.

### FACTFILE 1 — PURPOSE/AUDIENCE

PURPOSES FOR WRITING
You could be writing to:

| | | |
|---|---|---|
| inform | describe | reflect |
| explain | justify | instruct |
| narrate | evoke | tell |
| evaluate | analyse | comment |
| argue | report | persuade |

AUDIENCES FOR WRITING
You could be writing for:

| | | |
|---|---|---|
| yourself | a friend | your group or class |
| a teacher | parents | newspaper readers |
| people you don't know | | people who think like you |
| people in authority | | a mixture of these |

**1** With a partner, study the different samples of writing on these pages. For each one, try to decide on the form of the writing, the writer's purpose and the audience it is intended for.

**Ram Cuon**

Triangular deep-fried spring rolls

225g (8oz) minced beef
100g (4oz) bean sprouts
½ small onion, minced
25g (1oz) cellophane noodles, soaked for 20 minutes, drained and cut into small pieces
2 shallots or white parts of spring onions, chopped
2 gloves garlic, chopped
freshly ground black pepper
100g (40oz) white crabmeat, cooked and flaked
10 rice papers
2 eggs, beaten
10 raw prawns, shelled and de-veined
450ml (¾ pt) vegetable oil for frying

Prepare the filling by mixing together the beef, bean sprouts, onion, noodles, shallots, garlic, pepper and crabmeat.

Using one rice paper at a time, put on a flat surface and paint with beaten egg until softened. Fold one third of rice paper circle over, so you have a semi-circle with one straight edge. Put 2 tbs filling on the folded section, halfway along straight edge, and shape it into a square. Place a prawn on the filling, put another 2 tbs of filling on top of the prawn, and fold the sides of the rice paper over. Tuck in any ragged edges to give a neat triangular parcel, fastened by the egg. Fry the rolls, starting with the oil cold, bringing the heat to moderate. Fry for 30 minutes, until golden brown.

Serve with a vegetable platter (lettuce plus assortment of mint, coriander, dill, basil, bean sprouts sliced cucumber, spring onion etc.) and a spicy fish sauce.

Makes 10 spring rolls

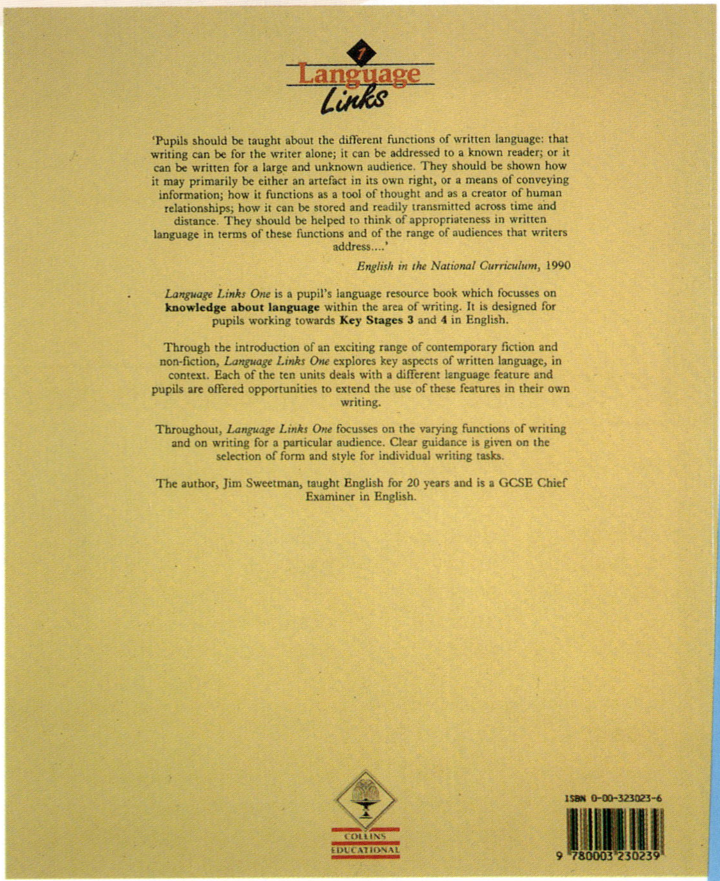

1 Language Links

'Pupils should be taught about the different functions of written language: that writing can be for the writer alone; it can be addressed to a known reader; or it can be written for a large and unknown audience. They should be shown how it may primarily be either an artefact in its own right, or a means of conveying information; how it functions as a tool of thought and as a creator of human relationships; how it can be stored and readily transmitted across time and distance. They should be helped to think of appropriateness in written language in terms of these functions and of the range of audiences that writers address....'

*English in the National Curriculum*, 1990

*Language Links One* is a pupil's language resource book which focusses on **knowledge about language** within the area of writing. It is designed for pupils working towards **Key Stages 3** and **4** in English.

Through the introduction of an exciting range of contemporary fiction and non-fiction, *Language Links One* explores key aspects of written language, in context. Each of the ten units deals with a different language feature and pupils are offered opportunities to extend the use of these features in their own writing.

Throughout, *Language Links One* focusses on the varying functions of writing and on writing for a particular audience. Clear guidance is given on the selection of form and style for individual writing tasks.

The author, Jim Sweetman, taught English for 20 years and is a GCSE Chief Examiner in English.

COLLINS EDUCATIONAL

ISBN 0-00-323023-6

9 780003 230239

## CHAPTER 1

Jake Shepherd sat completely motionless in the blue armchair. On a portable TV at his feet Wilma Flintstone was making omelettes with pterodactyl eggs. Jake smiled, then sneaked a glance at his watch. 'Mum,' he muttered, '– it's nearly six and you haven't even changed yet.'

No reply.

*'Mum?'*

'Nearly finished,' came an absorbed voice from across the chaotic, sunlit studio. For a moment there was nothing but a mixture of cartoon sound effects and distant traffic noise from Notting Hill Gate, then the voice resumed. 'I'm just doing your chin, all right? – so don't move a muscle for the next two minutes.'

Jake sighed. Now they were going to be late for the lower-sixth parents' 'do' at Portobello because of his chin. Groaning inwardly he began watching television again, deftly turning the sound up with socked foot as the six o'clock news came on. A bomb in Paris, the unemployment figures, a plane crash in Brazil, clips of a parliamentary debate, the F.T. Index, Charles and Diana at a film première – one by one the main stories flashed onto the screen accompanied by slick computer graphics and a stern voice-over.

'Doom, gloom and royals,' said Kay Shepherd, squinting abstractedly at her canvas. 'Is that really all that goes on in the world?' She stepped back and ran one hand down her paint-spattered smock. 'There. That's it for today. Want to have a look?'

Jake stretched with noisy relief and reached for the OFF button as his mother turned the easel round. Well, it was starting to look like him all right – even he could see the likeness now. She'd got the barber-proof blond cowlick, the angular, foxy outline of his face and

## Untitled

You are reading this too fast.
Slow down, for this is poetry
and poetry works slowly.
Unless you live with it a while
the spirit will never descend.
It's so easy to quickly cut across the surface
and then claim there was nothing to find.
Touch the poem gently with your eyes
just as you would touch a lover's flesh.
Poetry is an exercise in patience,
you must wait for it to come to you.
The spirit manifests in many guises,
some quiver with beauty,
some vibrate with song.
What is happening?
Slow down, slow down,
take a few deep breaths,
read the poem slowly,
read the lines one at a time,
read the words one by one,
read the spaces between the words,
get sleepy, this is poetry,
relax until your heart
is vulnerable, wide open.

*Ken Norris*

# Should I Be Registered for VAT?

Important Information on When and How to Apply

VAT

'X 430CD £450
ound quality, although player produced noticeable
l noise. Similar model: FX 430CDM with multiplay CD £500

JVC W23CD £330
Low priced. Fairly basic, but simple to u
player poorer than others. No tape aut

OD M-25CDS £400
good performance – if you want a record player in your
stem this is good value for money

PHILIPS F320CD £530
Simple to use once set up. Good Cl
separate mains leads

YING GUIDE

TEM
ood M-25CDS £400 did well all
etter speakers (around £100)
prove the sound further. For
sound quality, the Akai FX
50 is also worth considering.

TEM
he Technics SC-CH7 £500, with
CD sound quality and useful
The cheaper Sony MHC-1600CD
has many useful features and
ette sound quality.

Why is it bad to write on an empty stomach?
**Because paper is better!**

A teacher was finding out about her new class's abilities. 'Billy,' she asked, 'do you write with your left hand or your right hand?' Billy thought for a moment or two, and then said, 'Neither, Ms, I write with a pencil.'

**A:** **What are you doing?**
**B:** **Writing to my brother.**
**A:** **Don't be silly – you can't write!**
**B:** **So what? My brother can't read.**

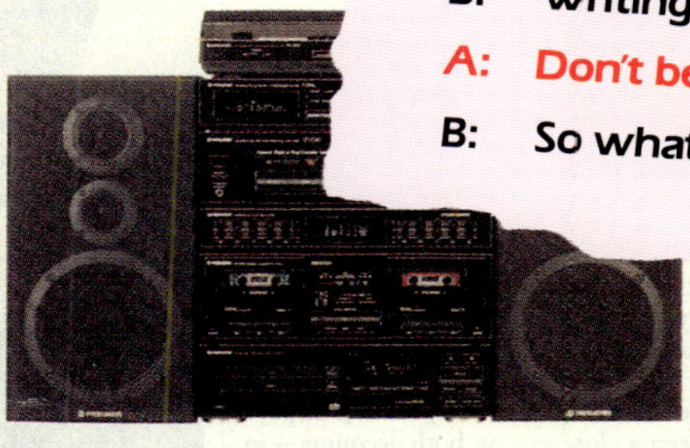

PIONEER S125 CDT £420
CD player takes two CDs, but fiddly to use. Record player sound

## YOUR OWN WRITING

**2** **Now, look closely at your own writing. Make your own full-page copy of the chart below to help you look back at the writing you have done recently in school. Work with a partner to complete the chart. For each subject, note down the last written task you were set and, using the factfile at the start of the unit, try to identify the audience and purpose of the writing. You may need to note down more than one purpose or audience.**

| SUBJECT | THE WRITING TASK (the title or instructions you were given) | THE WRITING PURPOSE (the type of writing) | THE AUDIENCE (the people who read it) |
|---|---|---|---|
| English | | | |
| Maths | | | |
| Science | | | |
| Technology | | | |
| Other subjects | | | |

## TYPES OF WRITING

In school, thinking about your task and its purpose may help you to decide on your audience. Knowing why you are writing and who you are writing for can also help you to decide on what *writing type* to use.

*Stories*, *accounts*, *comparisons*, *explanations* and *descriptions* are different types of writing. They each have their own characteristic features which help us to recognise them or to tell them apart. For example, if you read a letter from a friend one of the things that you are doing as you read is identifying the writing type. You will be expecting to find a conversational, chatty style, with simple description that you will both understand and references to people and places that you share which may be private and personal.

Although this letter might not make sense to most people, it does make sense for Jas and Pod. For them it is an effective communication which conveys a clear set of messages. If you write regularly to a good friend, you may well write in the same kind of way and your writing will have similar features.

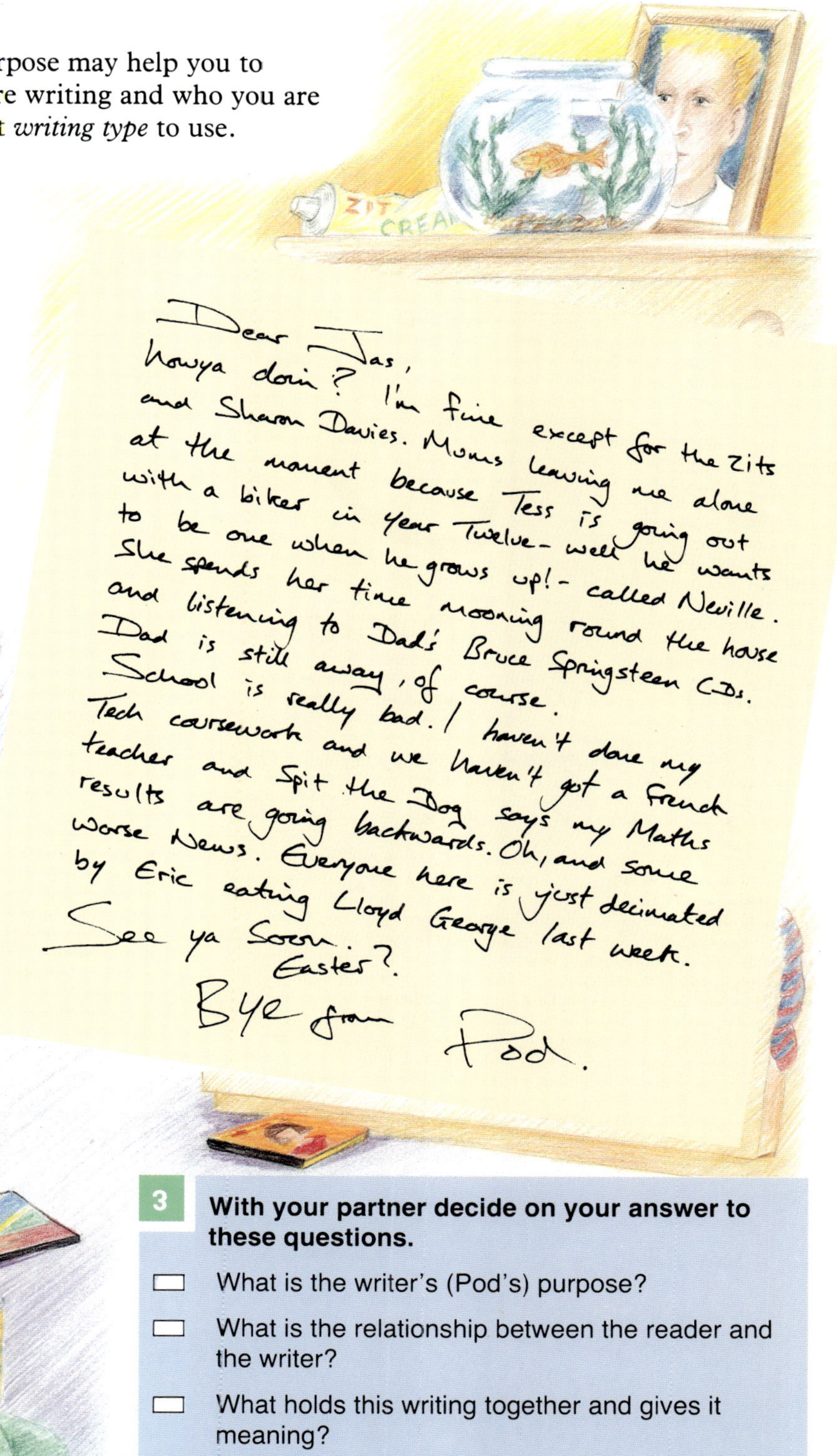


Dear Jas,
howya doin? I'm fine except for the zits and Sharon Davies. Mums leaving me alone at the moment because Tess is going out with a biker in Year Twelve - well he wants to be one when he grows up! - called Neville. She spends her time mooning round the house and listening to Dad's Bruce Springsteen CDs. Dad is still away, of course.
School is really bad. I haven't done my Tech coursework and we haven't got a French teacher and Spit the Dog says my Maths results are going backwards. Oh, and some worse News. Everyone here is just decimated by Eric eating Lloyd George last week.
See ya Soon.
Easter?
Bye from
Pod.

**3** **With your partner decide on your answer to these questions.**

- ☐ What is the writer's (Pod's) purpose?
- ☐ What is the relationship between the reader and the writer?
- ☐ What holds this writing together and gives it meaning?
- ☐ Why doesn't Pod write in Standard English? Should he?
- ☐ Why couldn't your coursework be written like this?
- ☐ Where could you write like this?

Sometimes at school you will be told what writing type or form to use and you will also be given an audience for it. You may be asked to write a story for children of a particular age, for example, or to write a letter to a newspaper. You will have to decide what features that writing should have to communicate its message.

Some of our knowledge of writing types comes with our first learning of language. Study the piece of writing below with a partner. Although Shawn is very young, it is already possible to identify some noticeable features in his writing.

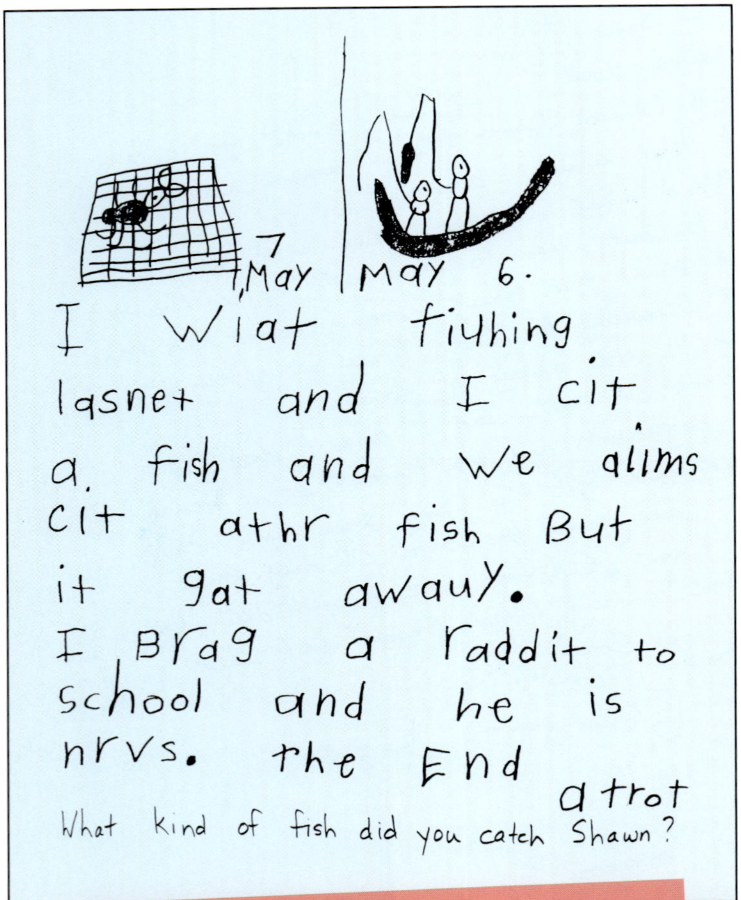
7 May | May 6.
I Wiat fiuhing
lasnet and I cit
a fish and we alims
cit athr fish But
it gat away.
I Brag a raddit to
school and he is
nrvs. the End
What kind of fish did you catch Shawn?
a trot

**May 7/May 6**

I went fishing
last night and I caught
a fish and we almost
caught another fish but
it got away.
I brang (brought) a rabbit to
school and he is
nervous. The End
(What kind of fish did you catch Shawn?)
A trout

**4 Discuss Shawn's writing with your partner. As you talk, think about:**

- ☐ the subject and content of the writing. Is the writing about Shawn or about fishing? Is the content concerned with 'I', the fishing trip or the rabbit? What does the writing concentrate on?
- ☐ who the writing is for. Is it for Shawn? His teacher? His parent? All of these?
- ☐ how the writing is held together or organised. You might spot the use of 'I' (the first person) throughout, the use of 'and' and 'but' (connectives) to link ideas and events, the date at the top and the use of 'the end' at the conclusion.

You and your partner can probably agree on a name for this form of writing. You might call it a 'diary entry' or a 'journal'. Shawn is already on his way to using a writing type which can help him express and communicate meanings to other people. When you look at other diary entries and journals, or write your own, you will probably find some of the same features.

## IN FOCUS

Much of the writing you are asked to do in school is about yourself and what you have seen or felt. Writing about personal experience is also the kind of writing you are most likely to write at home, in your diary or in letters to friends and relations.

Personal experiences provide a clear starting point for any writing where you and your reactions are the main focus for the writing. The *focus of the writing* is a term you will encounter throughout this book. It means the most important thing you have to bear in mind as you write. In Pod's letter (page 13), the reader – Jas – was the focus for the writing, but in Shawn's journal (opposite) the focus was on the events he was describing.

## *Diaries*

One way to record personal experience is in a diary. Most people have tried to keep a diary at one time or another. Some diaries have a very limited audience – the writer only – and are for the most private thoughts and feelings. On the other hand, journals such as those kept by explorers tend to be written for a wider audience.

2 September Lords day
By and by Jane comes and tells me that she hears that above 300 houses have been burned down tonight by the fire we saw and that it was now burning down all Fishstreet by London Bridge.

14 February 1910
There is no getting away from the fact that we are not pulling strong. Probably none of us: Wilson's leg still troubles him and he doesn't like to trust himself on ski; but the worst case is Evans, who is giving us serious anxiety. This morning he suddenly disclosed a huge blister on his foot...... Sometimes I fear he is going from bad to worse.

1861
Went over at 7 as I usually did. It was a bright morning; the sun just rising and shining brightly. Never can I forget how beautiful my darling looked lying there with his face lit by the rising sun... I took his hand which was already cold, though the breathing was quite gentle and I knelt down by him.

Jan 15: What a great weekend! Snowed all day Friday so on Saturday morning Grev and I took Blondie up to Campion Hills and went sledging with a fertiliser sack of his Dad's. I was petrified going down the big slope until I got used to it because other sledges had made the ice really smooth. It was well okay.

**LLAR-TO-POST COMPLAINT**

ave just read your article *Passing the parcels* in November's *hich?*, p612. I recently lost out as a result of a lost parcel. I felt at I was wrongly advised, and took the matter up with both rcelforce and Post Office Counters. The latter said that rcelforce were responsible because they had lost the parcel, d Parcelforce said that since Post Office Counters had lvised me incorrectly, I should pursue the matter with them.

As your survey showed, counter staff are not always able to ve correct advice concerning services of another business – arcelforce in this case. Both sides can so easily blame each ther, leaving the customer high and dry.

F KLAPTOCZ
Twickenham

*Now that the Post Office is split into three businesses (Royal Mail, Post Office Counters and Parcelforce), we're concerned hat customers may get the run-around. We plan to look more closely at the service you get from Post Office staff, and to sort out who's responsible when things go wrong.*

**WE'VE JUST SPLIT UP AND I CAN'T COPE**

**I am so miserable. My boyfriend of six months has just chucked me. I love him so much and I don't know what to do without him. I know there's no chance of us going out again because he's leaving town soon. I don't know how to cope without him; I feel useless and ugly. I also cry all the time and I hate going out. Why can't I get over him?**

**THOUGH few of us can afford a Rolls-Royce car, the possibility of the company being owned — even partly — by a foreign company is utterly appalling.**

**The Rolls-Royce is a part of our heritage and should be treated as such by the Government if it has a shred of patriotism. If British art treasures are in danger of being sold abroad there is always an outcry. There should be an even stronger one concerning the Rolls-Royce motor car firm.**

**RICHARD A. CATER,**
**Ipswich.**

PLEASE READ THIS LETTER VERY CAREFULLY. IT CONTAINS IMPORTANT INSTRUCTIONS AND INFORMATION RELATING TO YOUR AWARD IN THE FOLLOWING CATEGORIES:

| GOLD CATEGORY | SILVER CATEGORY | BRONZE CATEGORY |
|---|---|---|
| 1992 FORD ESCORT 1.6 GHIA OR BAHAMAS CRUISE AND STAY HOLIDAY OR £2,000 CASH | £250 CASH OR PORTABLE COLOUR T.V. WITH REMOTE CONTROL OR OLYMPUS CAMERA | MICROWAVE OVEN OR 5 PIECE TEFAL PRIMA COOKWARE OR £75 CASH |

**YOU ARE AN AWARD RECIPIENT IN THE GOLD CATEGORY**

Your unique no. 1139989 has unlocked the GOLD CATEGORY and you are guaranteed ONE AWARD in the category subject to the details of eligibility and conditions overleaf.

Your exact award is determined by matching your unique number with the Official Awards List at our exhibition centre.

Dear Gran,

Thanks for the record token. I got two others and I haven't spent them all yet. Are you enjoying the snow? Last Saturday I went tobogganing with my friend Greville and his dog Blondie – she's a Labrador – up on Campion Hills, the big hills at the back of the park. We had an ace time .....

Dear Points of View,

Why (oh why) can't 'Press Gang' be shown at a more sensible time? Twenty to five is much too early for me and my friends who travel on school buses. Then the repeats of the last series were shown on Sunday evenings. You keep telling us that it's an award-winning programme so let's see more of Linda Day and the team at a reasonable time of day.

Letters also can have very different audiences and purposes. You can write personal letters to friends and relatives, where the audience is limited to one other person. Or you can write letters to give your view, to seek for work and to ask for information – which are public. If you write a letter to a newspaper, then you hope that as many people as possible will read it and find out what you think.

**5** **Think of an event which has happened recently in your life. First, write a diary entry recording what happened – for yourself. Then write about the same event in a letter to a friend or a newspaper, television show or magazine. Compare your accounts within your group.**

### *Other writing*

Some people think more deeply about their past experiences and look back on their lives by writing an *autobiography*. They set out to describe the events which made them into the kinds of people they are.

Others may write *poems* to capture a particular emotion or feeling – perhaps a short-lived one – in writing. In these examples, the focus of the writing is to communicate information about the writer. The writing concentrates on the writer and on what happened to him or her.

However, there are other types of writing where *objective* observations and opinions are more important than *subjective* feelings and reactions. For example, in writing where you are describing your viewpoint, giving your opinion or arguing against someone else's ideas, the focus changes to become your views and how well you can support them.

Sometimes, the accuracy and precision of your observation is what matters. In writing about a reaction which took place during a scientific experiment, the *facts* about what you did and the *detailed description* of what you saw or what happened are most important.

On other occasions you may have to make judgements or assessments in writing. Here you may have to turn feelings and reactions into a *considered response*. You may be asked to *evaluate* evidence concerning an event in history or to sum up what was achieved by a field trip survey. You may have to *compare* books, plays and poems.

**6** **Look through a number of newspapers and magazines and collect together four or five different forms of writing. You should be able to find letters, news items, horoscopes, sports reports, editorials and reviews. Mount them on paper and then decide what you think are the focus, purpose and audience for each of them. Write a brief commentary to go with each one, giving your ideas.**

# KNOWLEDGE ABOUT LANGUAGE

For all these different forms of writing, the focus, purpose, and audience for the writing may vary. As they change to suit the writer's message, so does the language which is used. The choice and range of words (*vocabulary*) may be different, the way that the words are grouped into sentences or linked together in other ways (*grammar*) may alter and how the different parts of the writing are related into sections or paragraphs (*organisation*) can change as well. For example, in writing a report of a news event or an experiment, it is important to say what happened *chronologically* (in the order in which events took place). A chronological account will probably use words like 'then' or 'afterwards' to show that time is passing.

On the other hand, a description needs to group information differently and to link parts of the description together by relating them to one another. A description might use words like 'beneath' or 'above' (*prepositions*) to show how parts of the 'picture' being described combine together.

There again, a leaflet or a poster might use commands (*imperatives*) to attract people's attention or warn them of dangers.

POLICE are piecing together a description of the man. He is thought to be of medium build and under six feet tall. His hair is blond and he has a pale complexion. He has a scar under the right eye and the word HATE is tattooed across the knuckles of his right hand. He was wearing a black leather jacket over a white teeshirt, denim jeans and trainers.

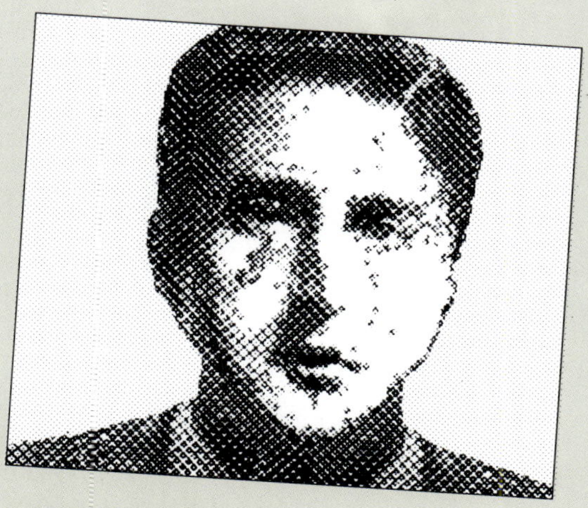

## HAVE YOU SEEN THIS MAN?

**A man with this appearance was involved in an armed raid on a shop last week. He is thought to be dangerous. If you see him, call the Police. Do not approach him.**

## FACTFILE 2

### A WRITING GLOSSARY

AUDIENCE
The person or people who are expected to read a piece of writing.

CHRONOLOGICAL ORDERING
Writing about events in the order in which they took place. Non-chronological ordering is the name used for writing which groups information in other ways.

FIRST PERSON
Using 'I' or 'We' and making the writer the focus of the writing.

FOCUS
The most important aspect of the writing – it can be the writer, the subject or the reader.

GRAMMAR
The different ways of using sentences and the correct ordering of verbs and nouns for effect.

IMPERATIVE
A verb form used to give orders – Do this! Go there!

OBJECTIVE STYLE
Writing which gives facts, says what things are like or reports events without the writer interrupting.

ORGANISATION
How the separate parts of a piece of writing are related or connected to one another.

PURPOSE
What the writing sets out to do, or the reason for doing it.

SUBJECTIVE STYLE
Writing which gives the writer's point of view.

THIRD PERSON
Making another person – 'he', 'she' or 'they' – the focus of the writing.

VOCABULARY
The ways that words are used in writing or how groups of words are used for effect.

## *'Here is the news . . .'*

With your group, read the news report below.

# KILLER DOGS ATTACK CHILDREN IN PARK

**A YOUNG girl was treated in hospital and five other children received attention for cuts and bruises after two bull terrier dogs escaped from a house in Whitnash Road on Thursday afternoon.**

The dogs ran through the park and attacked the children by the children's play area. The park supervisor, Jeremy Bigley, attempted to drive them off but was himself attacked. The child who was bitten, Abigail Terry, needed ten stitches for a wound on her face. Police rounded up the dogs and one of them was shot by a police marksman. The other was destroyed later.

The dog's owner, Shane Watkins (28), said that the dogs had never previously caused trouble and were always on a lead and muzzled when they were out. 'I can only think that someone opened my gate and let the dogs out deliberately,' he said later. 'The dogs are as good as gold and often play with my own children.'

**7 Each write one of the following:**

- ☐ Abigail Terry's account of what happened
- ☐ a letter from Shane Watkins to the local paper
- ☐ a formal police report on the incident
- ☐ a letter from a dog-lover to the local newspaper
- ☐ your own view of what happened and who was to blame
- ☐ an entry from Jeremy Bigley's diary written on the day of the attack.

**Afterwards, share and compare what you have written and see how your approaches to, and your ways of writing about, the same incident can be very different according to your purpose, the audience and the focus of your writing. Use the words in the factfile on page 21 to help you describe the differences between them.**

### ◆◆ *REWIND* ◆◆

- Think about writing types whenever you are asked to write or want to communicate in writing. Choose a writing type which fits the focus, purpose and audience for your writing.
- Learning about the features of different writing types can help you to decide on the best approach to a writing task.
- Knowing about writing types can help you use them more effectively and become a better writer.

# What happened?

## EYE-WITNESS ACCOUNT

A successful piece of writing matches focus, purpose, audience and language features to communicate a message most effectively. Any written message which makes sense to someone else contains information. This section and the next explore a range of writing types where the focus is on events and facts and whose purpose is to inform rather than to describe.

What happened? This is a question which is asked in all sorts of situations and places. It is one you will commonly be asked to answer in writing.

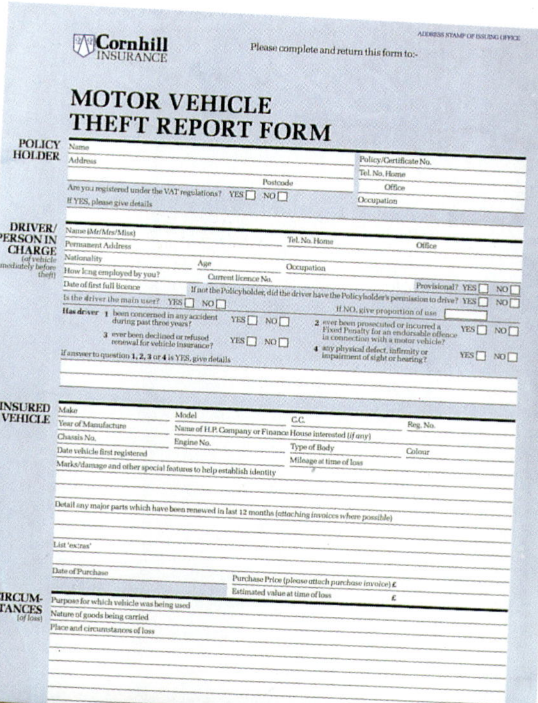

Cornhill INSURANCE

ADDRESS STAMP OF ISSUING OFFICE

Please complete and return this form to:-

**MOTOR VEHICLE THEFT REPORT FORM**

**POLICY HOLDER**
Name
Address
Postcode
Policy/Certificate No.
Tel. No. Home
Office
Occupation
Are you registered under the VAT regulations? YES ☐ NO ☐
If YES, please give details

**DRIVER/ PERSON IN CHARGE** (of vehicle immediately before theft)
Name (Mr/Mrs/Miss)
Tel. No. Home
Office
Permanent Address
Nationality
Age
Occupation
How long employed by you?
Current licence No.
Date of first full licence
Provisional? YES ☐ NO ☐
If not the Policyholder, did the driver have the Policyholder's permission to drive? YES ☐ NO ☐
Is the driver the main user? YES ☐ NO ☐
If NO, give proportion of use ☐
Has driver 1 been concerned in any accident during past three years? YES ☐ NO ☐
2 ever been prosecuted or incurred a Fixed Penalty for an endorsable offence in connection with a motor vehicle? YES ☐ NO ☐
3 ever been declined or refused renewal for vehicle insurance? YES ☐ NO ☐
4 any physical defect, infirmity or impairment of sight or hearing? YES ☐ NO ☐
If answer to question **1, 2, 3** or **4** is YES, give details

**INSURED VEHICLE**
Make
Model
C.C.
Reg. No.
Year of Manufacture
Name of H.P. Company or Finance House interested (*if any*)
Chassis No.
Engine No.
Type of Body
Colour
Date vehicle first registered
Mileage at time of loss
Marks/damage and other special features to help establish identity
Detail any major parts which have been renewed in last 12 months (*attaching invoices where possible*)
List 'extras'
Date of Purchase
Purchase Price (*please attach purchase invoice*) £
Estimated value at time of loss £

**CIRCUM-STANCES** (*of loss*)
Purpose for which vehicle was being used
Nature of goods being carried
Place and circumstances of loss

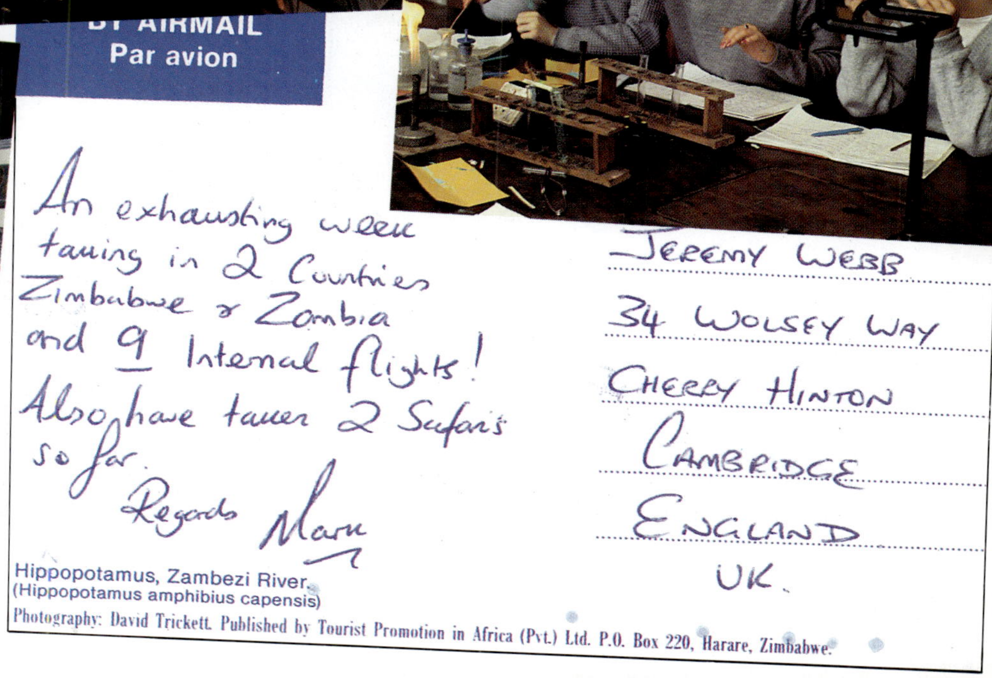

BY AIRMAIL
Par avion

An exhausting week taking in 2 Countries Zimbabwe & Zambia and 9 Internal flights! Also have taken 2 Safari's so far.
Regards Mark

JEREMY WEBB
34 WOLSEY WAY
CHERRY HINTON
CAMBRIDGE
ENGLAND
UK.

Hippopotamus, Zambezi River.
(Hippopotamus amphibius capensis)
Photography: David Trickett. Published by Tourist Promotion in Africa (Pvt.) Ltd. P.O. Box 220, Harare, Zimbabwe.

## EYE WITNESS

Writing down what happened in a particular situation or as a chain of events unfolded is not difficult. Most of the conversations we have with other people give an account of events in this way. Many of the novels and stories you read do the same. Newspaper reports say what happened, when it took place and who was involved. Letters to friends, relatives or penpals tell them what has happened recently in our own lives, and so on.

In school, you are often asked to write in this way. You might be asked to write about what happened on a field trip or excursion; to say what you noticed as you watched a scientific experiment, or studied the performance of a model you had made as part of a technology course. You might be asked to relate a sequence of historical events or an episode from a play or story as if you were present at the time.
You could be asked to:

**give an eye-witness account**

**make a statement**

**recount the events**

**give a personal account**

**report back to the class**

**describe what you saw and did**

As an adult, you may find yourself doing the same. For example, if the company you work for asks for a report on your recent sales trip; if you witness a crime; if you are involved in a traffic incident; when you write letters home from college or postcards from abroad you will still be writing about, and focusing on, what happened.

### *Did he see it?*

Read the two eye-witness accounts (on pages 25 and 26). The first concerns a sighting of the Loch Ness Monster in 1934 by J W Fraser and the second is taken from a police report of a UFO sighting in 1964.

## SIGHTING ONE

'Towards the end of June 1934 I was approached by a representative of Sir Edward Mountain who had taken over Beaufort Castle from Lord Loost for the salmon fishing. I was asked if I would like to take charge of some men he intended to place round Loch Ness with cameras to see if they could find evidence of an unusual animal that had been seen from time to time by locals and visitors. Twenty men were engaged and I placed them at strategic points on both sides of the Loch, 14 men on the North side and six on the South side. Several snaps had been taken but there was not sufficient evidence to establish the identity of the animal. The search was continued for about six weeks when the men were withdrawn.

Sir Edward then asked me if I would stay on with one man to carry on the search. This I did, which meant that I had to take up residence, which I also did - in a bell tent on the hill above Urquhart Castle. The procedure I adopted was at dawn I took up my stance at the roadside to the East of the Castle. I had with me a 16mm cine camera; also a pair of powerful binoculars. I was relieved for meals by my assistant.

One Saturday, about midway through August, I took my usual stance at dawn. There was that morning a thick haze hanging over the Loch, it afterwards turned out to be a very hot day. I carried out my usual procedure, that was to scan the Loch westwards then turn to scan the Loch eastwards; then to my surprise I observed what I thought was a rock about 100 yards from the shore East of the Urquhart Bay. This object which appeared inanimate I had under observation for over a minute, then I remembered that there was no rock that far out from the shore. I then took up my camera and trained it on this object and started to film it, when to my surprise the object raised out of the water either its head and neck or a flipper, then lowered it, raising quite a volume of water, then it disappeared.

I then phoned Sir Edward Mountain who laid on a car to take the camera to Inverness and have the film taken out by a competent person and have it carefully packed and sent registered parcel service to Kodak. The train was met in London and the film taken to their laboratory and developed.'

SIGHTING TWO

Place: Socorro, New Mexico, USA
Date: 24 April 1964
Time: 17:45

I was pursuing a speeding automobile out in the desert when I was distracted by a sudden roar and a bluish flame in the sky ahead. I left the road and drove up a rough track where I spotted what I thought was an overturned car about 150 metres off the road.

As I came closer I saw it was an oval, silvery object on four feet. It was marked with a red insignia. Two small human-like objects wearing garments similar to overalls moved round near the object.

I approached them but they saw me and appeared alarmed. They then jumped into the craft, there was a roar and a brilliant blue flash as the object rose into the air. I was scared of the roar. Then I looked up and saw the object going away from me. The roar stopped. I heard a whine, then complete silence.

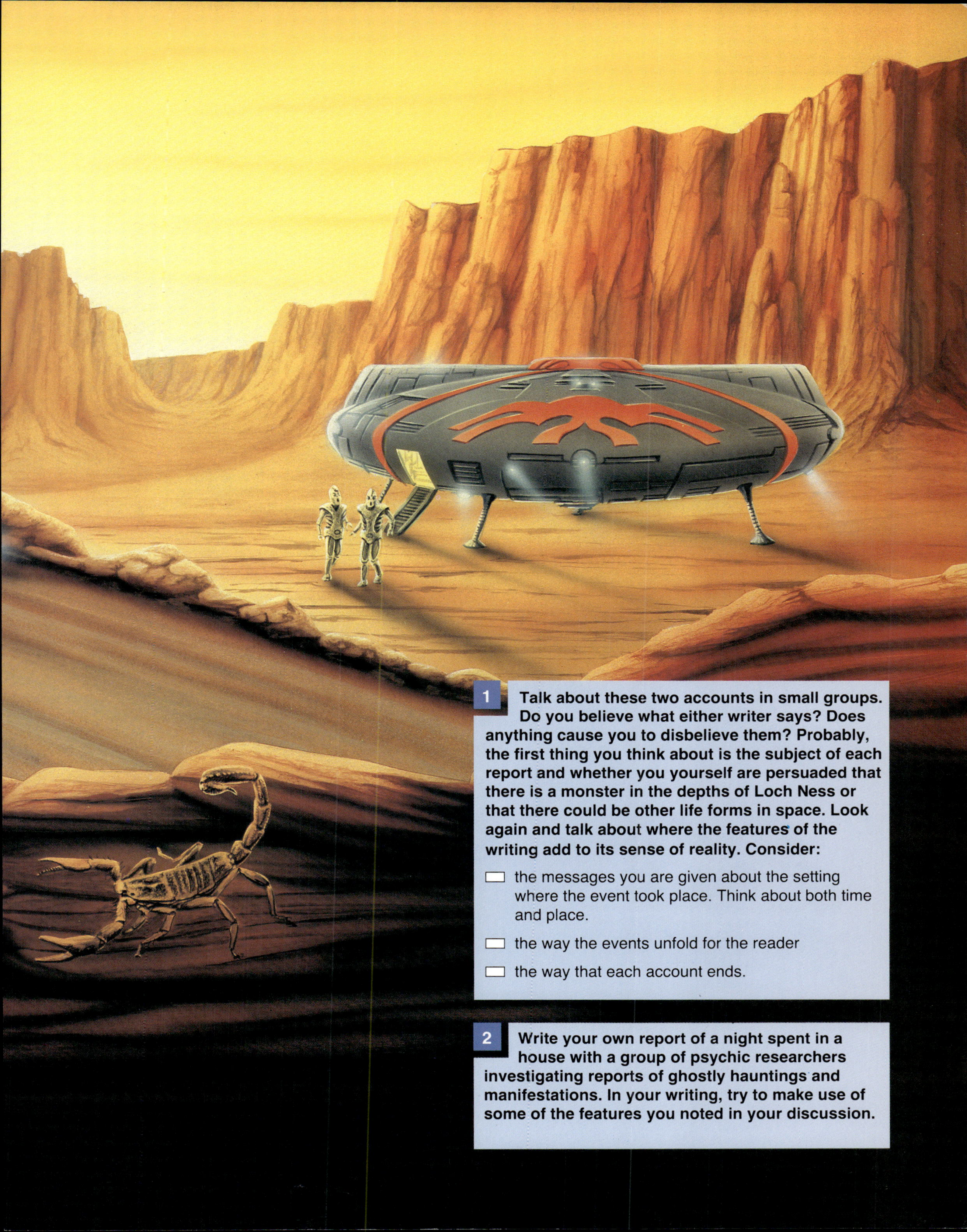

**1** **Talk about these two accounts in small groups. Do you believe what either writer says? Does anything cause you to disbelieve them? Probably, the first thing you think about is the subject of each report and whether you yourself are persuaded that there is a monster in the depths of Loch Ness or that there could be other life forms in space. Look again and talk about where the features of the writing add to its sense of reality. Consider:**

- ☐ the messages you are given about the setting where the event took place. Think about both time and place.
- ☐ the way the events unfold for the reader
- ☐ the way that each account ends.

**2** **Write your own report of a night spent in a house with a group of psychic researchers investigating reports of ghostly hauntings and manifestations. In your writing, try to make use of some of the features you noted in your discussion.**

# ANALYSING A WRITING TASK

So what have these kinds of writing got in common? When you 'report the facts' in different situations, for all sorts of reasons and for audiences which range from you and your class to almost anyone, what similar features does that writing have?

# Ban on trade in leopard skins may be lifted

**Polly Ghazi**

## Poachers could wipe out endangered cheetahs

A GLOBAL ban on trade in leopard skins may be lifted next month, boosting the flagging fur industry and raising fears that Africa's big cats will again fall prey to a poaching epidemic.

With the number of leopards increasing in Botswana, Malawi, Namibia, Zambia and Zimbabwe, the countries want to end a 17-year ban on commercial trade in their fur and export 2,000 skins a year.

The request t... vive the ...tive trad...

this week to urge Environment Secretary Michael Heseltine to oppose the move.

The Government has said it supports the 'sustainable utilisation' of wildlife, which implies it would agree to limited trade in protected wild animals whose numbers are growing.

'Britain must take the lead in resisting these disastrous pro-...als,' ...id Carol Mc...

coats remain popular, including Japan, Italy, Spain and America, where the industry has an annual turnover of $1 billion. Even in Britain, where the anti-fur campaign has had most effect, fake spotted-cat coats have recently become very fash-...

The demand to reopen the leopard-skin trade is one of several controversial southern African proposals that threaten to undermine the conservation basis of the United Nations wildlife convention.

Others, almost certain to be thrown out, include lifting trade bans on products from the highly endangered black rhinoceros and cheetah.

Southern African nations led ...

---

Fault Finding

Anna Potnis
10th October

...ntroduction Imagine there is a two-core cable stretching from a power station at one end to a village at the other - the cable is underground and develops a fault: eg. a short circuit, somewhere along the line.

...im Design 2 electrical circuits which will enable you to find the fault without digging up all the cable. This is represented in the lab by a model fault finding apparatus:

(Top view)

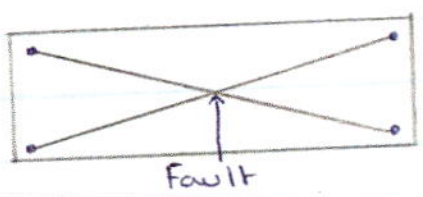


We must find the position of the fault.

---

...here we were standing in front of "The Linley Sisters" ... the Dulwich Picture Gallery – listening to sir droning ... and on – when suddenly he was there before us. ...e" was an actor dressed as Thomas Gainsborough. ... was wearing a fancy, full-length coat and ...rrying this really long paintbrush. This was ...ed to paint the background of portraits. "Thomas ...insborough" told us about the sisters in the ...inting – how one of them eloped with Sheridan ...e playwright. The actor also gave us some ...nts about the painter's painting techniques.

---

**3** **With a partner, look at the children's story, news item, account of a day out and the laboratory report. Decide between you what features they have in common? As you study each one, think about:**

- ☐ the *focus* of the writing. Is the writing's main focus on the subject – what happened – or on the part played by the writer?
- ☐ the *purpose* of the writing. What is the writing setting out to achieve? Why was it written?
- ☐ the *audience* for the writing. Who is meant to read the account? The writer? The people who were there? People who were not there? A specific group of people?
- ☐ the *order* in which events are recounted and how the writing is *organised*. Are events grouped together or recounted one after another?
- ☐ the *tense* of the writing. Are these events described as if they happened in the past, are taking place in the present or will take place in the future?

**Report back your findings to the group or class and see how far different pairs agree.**

**4** **As your next assignment, find other examples of a news story, a laboratory report and a children's story. Add an account of a day out written by yourself. Then write your own analysis of what *they* have in common using these headings to help you.**

**FOCUS PURPOSE AUDIENCE ORDER TENSE**

## SAME EVENT – DIFFERENT STORIES

Now, read the following report of a traffic accident. It contains the kind of details which drivers involved in accidents have to give when they claim compensation from an insurance company.

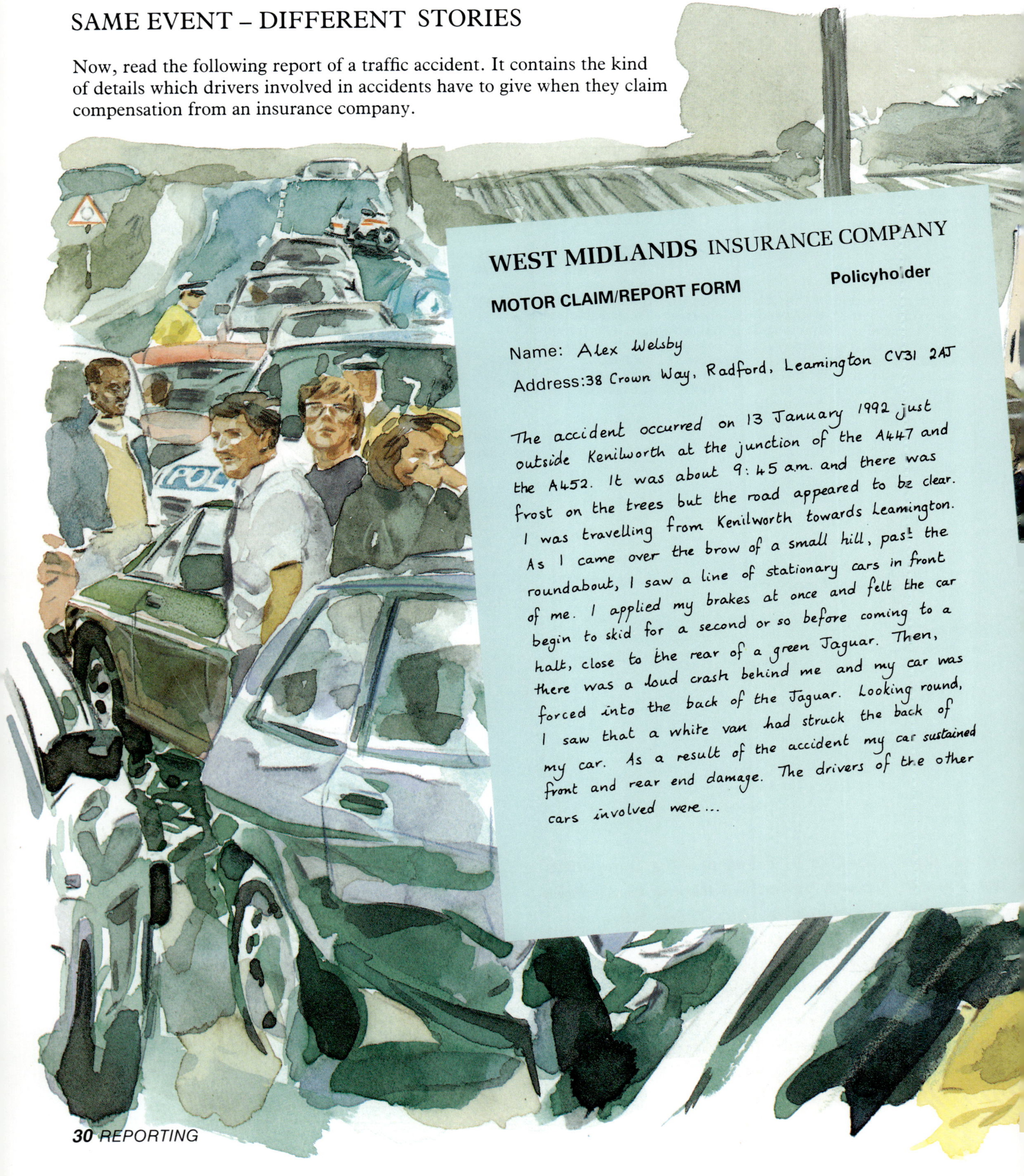

**WEST MIDLANDS** INSURANCE COMPANY

**MOTOR CLAIM/REPORT FORM** **Policyholder**

Name: Alex Welsby

Address: 38 Crown Way, Radford, Leamington CV31 2AJ

The accident occurred on 13 January 1992 just outside Kenilworth at the junction of the A447 and the A452. It was about 9:45 am. and there was frost on the trees but the road appeared to be clear. I was travelling from Kenilworth towards Leamington. As I came over the brow of a small hill, past the roundabout, I saw a line of stationary cars in front of me. I applied my brakes at once and felt the car begin to skid for a second or so before coming to a halt, close to the rear of a green Jaguar. Then, there was a loud crash behind me and my car was forced into the back of the Jaguar. Looking round, I saw that a white van had struck the back of my car. As a result of the accident my car sustained front and rear end damage. The drivers of the other cars involved were ...

**5** **Make a copy of the chart below. With your partner, complete the chart to analyse the main features of this eye-witness account. Use quotations or references to back up what you write in each section.** NOTE: The 'other features' section is where you can identify other things about the organisation of the writing or its use of vocabulary which you have noticed. Below, the 'Other features' section is completed for you.

| EYE-WITNESS ACCOUNT | FEATURE | EXAMPLE |
|---|---|---|
| **Subject**<br>What is the writing about? People, things, ideas? | | |
| **Purpose**<br>What is the writer's aim or goal? How can you tell what it is? | | |
| **Audience**<br>Who is the writing for? What kind of relationship is there between the writer and the reader(s)? Friendly? Polite? Formal? | | |
| **Organisation**<br>How is the writing ordered and structured? What makes it hold together? | | |
| **Tense**<br>What tenses are used – present/ future or past? | | |
| **Other features**<br>What do the vocabulary and grammar of the writing reveal about it? | 1) connectives are used to do with time<br>2) the sentences are quite short and often repeat the word 'I'<br>3) the writing is mostly factual and doesn't give opinions<br>4) there is a lot of specific detail | 'as', 'then'<br>'I was travelling from Kenilworth to Leamington.'<br>'13 January'<br>'A452'<br>'a green Jaguar' |

## RECOGNISING A WRITING TYPE

Features like the ones you identified on page 31 are what tell you, when you encounter a piece of writing for the first time, exactly what writing type it is. In this case, you could describe the writing type as an eye-witness report or as a *personal account*.

**6** **On these pages are four other pieces of writing based on the eye-witness account of events given on page 30. With a partner, try to give these writing types a name and, using the checklist of features on page 31, say how they differ from the eye-witness account.**

**A**

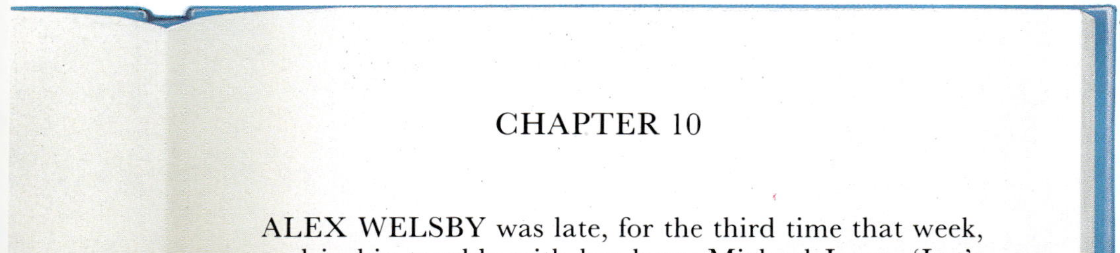

CHAPTER 10

ALEX WELSBY was late, for the third time that week, and in big trouble with her boss, Michael Joyce. 'Let's hope and pray he's later than me,' she thought, as she eased the XR3 off the roundabout away from the traffic and let her foot move towards the floor. The engine responded with a satisfying roar as she eased through the gears on the shallow gradient ahead. 'This is better,' she muttered as she thought back to the events of yesterday and the argument with Jackie while the sunlight filtered brightly through the frosted trees at the side of the road. Then, it seemed without any warning, there were swerving brilliant red lights ahead and the screeching of brakes in front and behind. The impact was sudden and it felt expensive. But that wasn't all. The tall figure climbing from the limousine in front to stare at the broken lights and dented bumper was one she knew at once. She would recognise Michael Joyce anywhere.

131

**B**

13th January.

A dreadful day. Smashed the car up on the way to Leamington. One of those thats no one's fault so I'll probably lose my no-claims discount as well as being off the road for the rest of the week. It would happen now as well, when I've got my local tax instalment and the down payment on the video to pay this month.

C

# SPUDS MAKE JAM

BLACK ice was described as the cause of a three-car pile-up outside Kenilworth which held up traffic on the A452 for two hours on Tuesday. The drivers were not injured but a pick-up van containing potatoes was involved and several sacks of potatoes were tipped into the roadway. Local firefighters and onlookers cleared them.

D

Sharpe & Donewell
Solicitors
11 Castle Drive
Kenilworth
CV34 2DQ

38 Crown Way,
Radford,
Leamington
CV31 2AJ

17 March 1992

Dear Sirs,

With reference to your letter dated 12 March 1992, I would like to make it clear that I accept absolutely no responsibility for the accident which took place on 13 January.

In my view, your client, Mr M Joyce, had halted suddenly in a dangerous position and the bright sunlight made his brake lights, if they were working at the time, hard to see.

Nevertheless, I was able to stop which was an achievement in itself since the road was icy. It was the impact from a following vehicle which caused my car to strike your client's.

I would suggest that you contact the driver of that vehicle as I have done and stop bothering me on this matter. The accident has caused me quite enough trouble and expense and I am very busy with a new job which I have only recently started.

Yours faithfully,

A. Welsby

## EYE-WITNESS ACCOUNTS

From your analysis and discussion, you should now be able to identify the main features of writing which reports on events, or presents your own account of something you have seen. The factfile on this page sums them up for you.

This kind of writing is very common. As you read more widely and write about more difficult subjects, you will realise that much of the writing, and many of the writing tasks, you encounter expect you to write like this. Studying these eye-witness or personal accounts shows you a *way of looking* at any type of writing and at how it is usually written. As you go on to explore other writing types or have to write in other ways, this approach will often help you to see what you are being asked to do.

Sometimes your writing may involve more than one type of writing or place a particular emphasis on one aspect of the writing. Perhaps you will be giving a mixture of factual report and personal opinion, or your report will cover a series of linked events and read like a group of mini-reports.

### FACTFILE 3 — REPORTING

When you report on events where you were present or give an eye-witness account remember that:

- the *focus* is on you, the writer, and what you observed is the most important part of the writing;
- the *purpose* of the writing is to *inform* others;
- your *audience* can be anyone who was not present;

AND

- the setting or background should be described;
- events should be recounted chronologically (the order in which they occurred);
- the past tense should be used to show when the events took place;
- specific factual details should be included.

**7** **Write TWO of the following:**

- ☐ An *eye-witness account* of a crime you witnessed while working at a local superstore. Focus on the time, the place, what you saw in detail, the sequence of events and so on.
- ☐ A *report* of a recent public or sporting event you watched, live or on television. Focus on the single occasion and on what happened.
- ☐ A *factual account* of something you have done recently in school. It might be a science experiment or investigation, a survey or field study or an assignment in Technology or another subject. Focus on the ordering of events and your observations.

**Once you have drafted and revised your writing, write a short commentary stating what you have learned about these writing types and assessing how well you think you did in using them.**

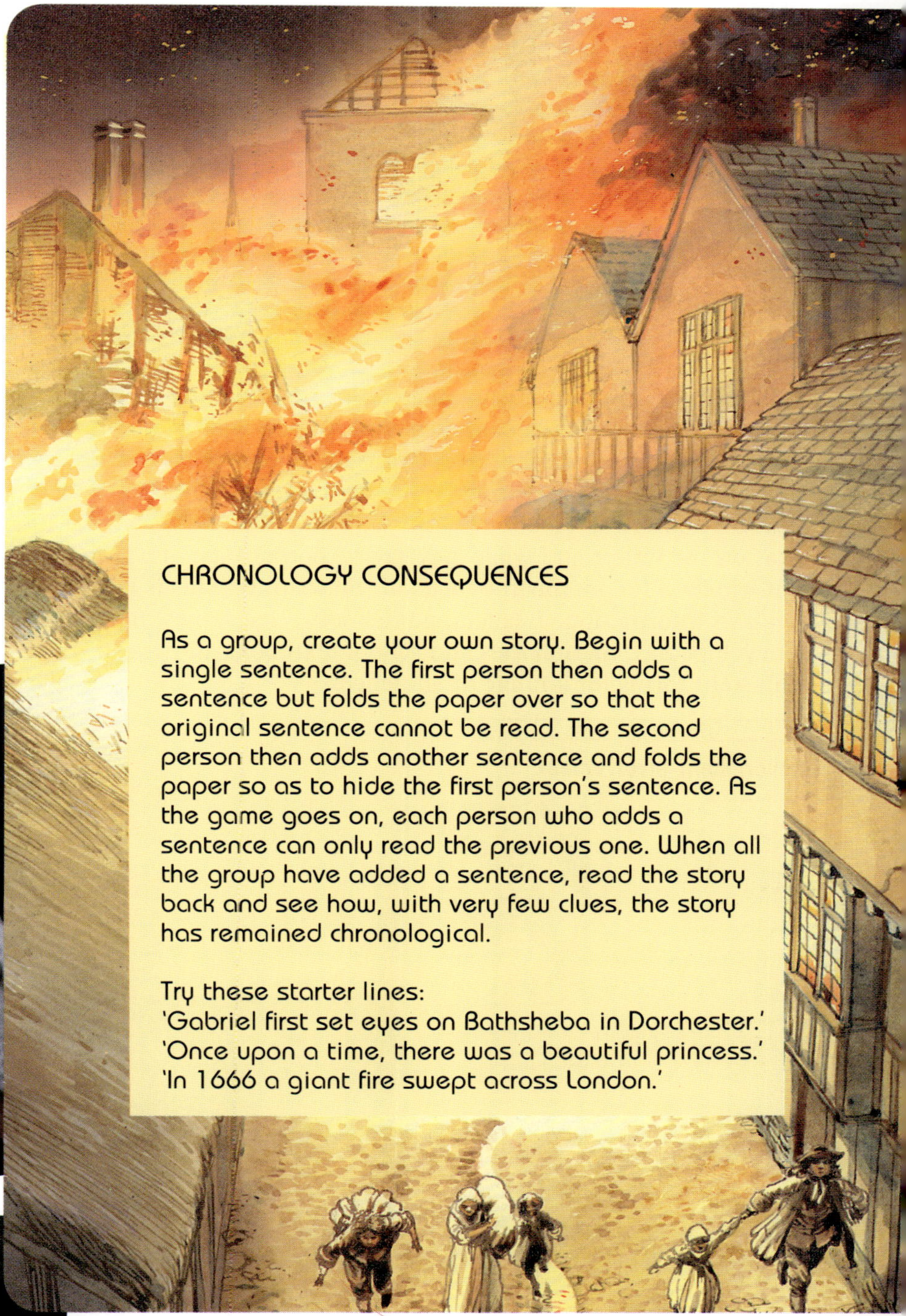

## CHRONOLOGY CONSEQUENCES

As a group, create your own story. Begin with a single sentence. The first person then adds a sentence but folds the paper over so that the original sentence cannot be read. The second person then adds another sentence and folds the paper so as to hide the first person's sentence. As the game goes on, each person who adds a sentence can only read the previous one. When all the group have added a sentence, read the story back and see how, with very few clues, the story has remained chronological.

Try these starter lines:
'Gabriel first set eyes on Bathsheba in Dorchester.'
'Once upon a time, there was a beautiful princess.'
'In 1666 a giant fire swept across London.'

### REWIND

- An eye-witness account presents the facts about an event in the order in which they took place.
- You are most likely to be asked to write eye-witness accounts in English, Science, Geography and Technology.
- You will often find eye-witness reporting linked to another writing type in a particular task.

3

# For your information

## PRESENTING INFORMATION

How does smoking damage your lungs? What is global warming? When does the bus go? What are my rights? These are all questions which seek information – facts, dates, times, definitions, reasons, laws and directions.

All writing communicates a range of information and messages. A story describes fictional events, a playscript says something about the characters in it, and an essay might put forward a student's views. This is all information. The eye-witness accounts you considered in the last section included information about events and situations; the focus of the writing was on the writer and what they saw. Another type of writing makes the information it contains the focus of the writing. This is writing which *presents* information. Leaflets, guidebooks, magazines, newspapers, encyclopedias, dictionaries and school textbooks all present information in different forms for a range of audiences.

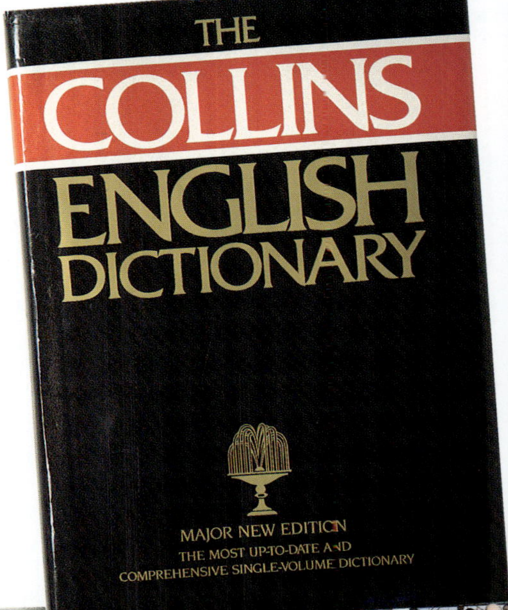

## FORMS AND GENRE

To go on to study these kinds of writing, it will be helpful to understand some of the words which language experts use. In the last section you studied a number of eye-witness reports – the type of informational writing which presents facts about events. Separate writing types, such as informational, are often referred to as *genres* (from the French word for 'type'). Persuasive writing, descriptive writing and narrative are some of the other writing genres you will encounter in this book. Each of them can be recognised by its particular purpose and by the different ways in which it uses language.

Another way of labelling writing is by its *form*. Letters, leaflets, posters, diary entries, advertisements, playscripts and poems are all different forms of writing. Forms are the possible 'shapes' of written texts. Whenever you attempt a writing task you probably combine a particular genre, an audience and a specific form. A writing form on its own is like an empty box or a design template, but the choice of audience and genre is what gives your writing its meaning.

**GENRE**

- informing
- persuading
- describing
- reflecting
- explaining
- instructing
- analysing
- comparing
- narrating

**FORM**

- paragraphs
- letter
- news article
- list
- diary
- poem
- leaflet
- poster
- playscript

**AUDIENCE**

- friend or relative
- expert
- yourself
- police officer
- newspaper reader
- anyone
- a teacher
- a child
- people who think like you

**1** **With a partner, study the three lists which show a range of genres, forms and audiences.**

☐ **Choose a word from each list to sum up what you are doing when you write:**

— to a local newspaper to ask people to support your campaign for a new youth club
— a poem based on a story that you have read in class
— exactly what your grandmother has to do to video a television programme for you
— a message to say where you'll meet your penpal
— the text to go with a technology display showing how a canal lock works.

☐ **Now use a word from each list to describe the following:**

— a recipe in a cordon bleu cookery book
— an entry in a hotel guide
— a postcard from your cousin
— a political message from the Green Party about recycling rubbish
— a technological study of alternative ways of designing toddlers' pushchairs
— a conclusion to a laboratory report about why an experiment failed.

**Compare your findings with the rest of your group.** Don't be surprised if you disagree. Experts argue about how many writing genres there are and there are other possible forms of writing and potential audiences. What matters is thinking about the different ways you might approach or revise a writing task.

# ANALYSING A WRITING GENRE – INFORMATION

In school, you will often be asked to give information as a way of showing that you understand or know about something you have been taught. Sometimes, you will be asked to apply that information to a new set of problems rather than merely presenting it, but very often it is the information itself with which you are concerned. You could be asked to:

*Present the facts about . . .*

*Describe a process . . .*

*Write a leaflet . . .*

*Say what you know about . . .*

*Provide information . . .*

*Write a report on . . .*

Informational writing comes in many forms. The examples on pages 39 to 43 show some of the many ways in which you may encounter writing which is, first and foremost, concerned with information.

**2** **Working with a partner, compare and contrast three examples of informational writing from these pages. Decide what features they have in common. Start by thinking about the features you considered in the previous section and your answers to these questions.**

- ☐ What is the *focus* of the writing? Is the writing's main focus on the subject and facts connected with it, or on a series of events, or on the part played by the writer?
- ☐ What is the *purpose* of the writing? Is it the same?
- ☐ Who is the *audience* for the writing? Who is meant to read this information – the writer, experts, or a specific group of people?
- ☐ How is the writing *organised*? Is the information given chronologically or grouped in some other way?
- ☐ What *tense* is used for the writing? Is the information given about things as if they exist in the present, happened in the past, or will exist in the future?

As you talk, you should begin to become aware of some of the main features of this kind of informational writing. You may also see how informational writing differs from an eye-witness account. **Report back your findings to the group and see how far different pairs agree.**

## FEVER FACTS

Over five million people suffer from hayfever in this country every year and the number is said to be rising. Also, it's said to affect those between the ages of 15 and 25 the most, which is bad news when it comes to exam time.

Until recently, long-term sufferers were given 'de-sensitising' injections, but now doctors prefer not to do this because of the possible side effects. Also, anybody who's had to take antihistamines to ease hayfever will know they can make you drowsy and less alert.

So, what is a hayfever sufferer to do? Well, those brill natural health people at New Era Laboratories have come up with New Era Combination H Homeopathically Prepared Mineral Tissue Salts.

They come in tablet-type form and work by redressing the balance of salts already present in the body. Three of the 12 mineral tissue salts found in the body have been included in Combination H to help relieve hayfever symptoms – running eyes, itching nose and constant sneezing.

It's recommended that you take them every day at least a month before the hayfever season starts to help build up the body's immune system – and that's without any nasty side effects. You can buy New Era tissue salts from most chemists and health food stores.

## MONTSERRAT

Located in the Leeward Islands, 27 miles/43 km southwest of Antigua, Montserrat is a mountainous volcanic island of 39.5 square miles/102 square km. A narrow belt of lowlands and foothills rises quickly to an interior highland green with rain forest and tropical vegetation and carved by rivers and streams. The central spine of mountains, formed as a result of three different volcanic eruptions, reaches its highest point in the south where cloud-wreathed Chance Peak rises from the Soufriere Hills and continuing volcanic activity is very much in evidence.

Montserrat was discovered by Columbus in 1493. As the story goes, the great explorer, upon seeing the island's serrated peaks, named it after the monastery of Santa Maria de Montserrat near Barcelona, which is surrounded by similar mountains. The Spanish apparently had no interest in the island, and the hills and forests were left to the Carib Indians until 1632 when the Irish arrived. The British and French fought over the island for a century or more, but finally, in 1783, the British acquired Montserrat and the island remains a British Crown Colony to this day.

In Montserrat's rich volcanic soil, sugarcane flourished and a plantocracy based on the labour of African slaves developed. After emancipation early in the nineteenth century and the decline of the sugar industry on the island, limes and later sea island cotton were cultivated as cash crops. Today, most of the lowlands that were once agricultural estates are covered with scrub and grassland, but in recent years cotton has made something of a comeback and the Montserrat government is committed to developing a local textile industry. Otherwise there is surprisingly little commercial agriculture, given the island's fertility and abundance of tropical fruits.

From the experience of touring the countryside and hiking through rain forests to waterfalls and volcanic peaks, it will be obvious that Montserrat has a rich variety of trees and plants typical of other islands in the eastern Caribbean. The lobster claw is the national flower, while many varieties of hibiscus, bougainvillea, anthuriums, ginger, and frangipani are common in gardens. Wild orchids, frequently found in the lower forests, can also be seen in local gardens and resort grounds, with the showiest being the yellow oncidiums. But the most impressive forms of vegetation on the island are the dense, huge tree ferns and the giant philodendrons called elephant ears in the rain forest.

## Tobacco

Tobacco is the dried leaves of a plant that grows in many parts of the world (it will even grow in England). Most tobacco is sold in the form of cigarettes. Cigars are made from stronger, darker tobacco rolled up in tobacco leaves, and this stronger tobacco can also be smoked in a pipe.

### Legal status

Selling tobacco to children under 16 is prohibited. Apart from this there are no restrictions on sale, other than that the taxes should have been paid; even children who cannot legally be *sold* tobacco, can legally buy, possess, and smoke it.

Control over the availability of tobacco is mainly through the effect of taxation on price, obviously a factor in how much will be bought and by whom. Currently taxes account for nearly three-quarters of the price of a typical packet of cigarettes.

### Prevalence and availability

Many tobacconists are unaware of the ban on sales to under-16s, and surveys have shown that nearly 85% would sell cigarettes to children obviously under-age.

About a quarter of 14–15 year-olds smoke at least a cigarette a week; amongst older teenagers, about 30% smoke, each smoker consuming on average 11–12 cigarettes a day. Overall, about 34% of the adult population are smokers; 1 in 5 men and 1 in 10 women smoke twenty or more a day.

### Short-term use

Cigarette smoke consists of droplets of tar, nicotine, carbon monoxide and other gases. How much of the nicotine (the main active ingredient) and these other substances is absorbed through the lungs depends on how much smoke is actually inhaled rather than 'puffed'. Pharmacologically, nicotine is a stimulant, and smokers can effectively use smoking to maintain performance in the face of fatigue and monotony. However, smoking is also used to alleviate stress and anxiety. The effects are practically immediate but rapidly decline, encouraging frequent use. Many people who smoke regularly say they find it relaxing and yet stimulating at the same time, and experience great satisfaction on inhaling. First-time users often feel sick and dizzy.

### Long-term use

The more a person smokes, the more likely they are to suffer from heart disease, blood clots, heart attacks, lung infections, strokes, bronchitis, bad circulation, lung cancer, cancer of the mouth and throat, and ulcers. Tobacco contributes to at least 100,000 premature deaths in the UK every year. On average, each cigarette is said to shorten the life of an habitual smoker by 5½ minutes.

Women who smoke a lot during pregnancy tend to have smaller babies and run a greater risk of losing the baby before or shortly after birth.

The most striking aspect of cigarette use is the extent of dependence and regular use. People who begin to smoke usually go on to smoke regularly. If they stop, they may feel restless, irritable and depressed, wanting another cigarette. More people are regular users of tobacco than of any other drug.

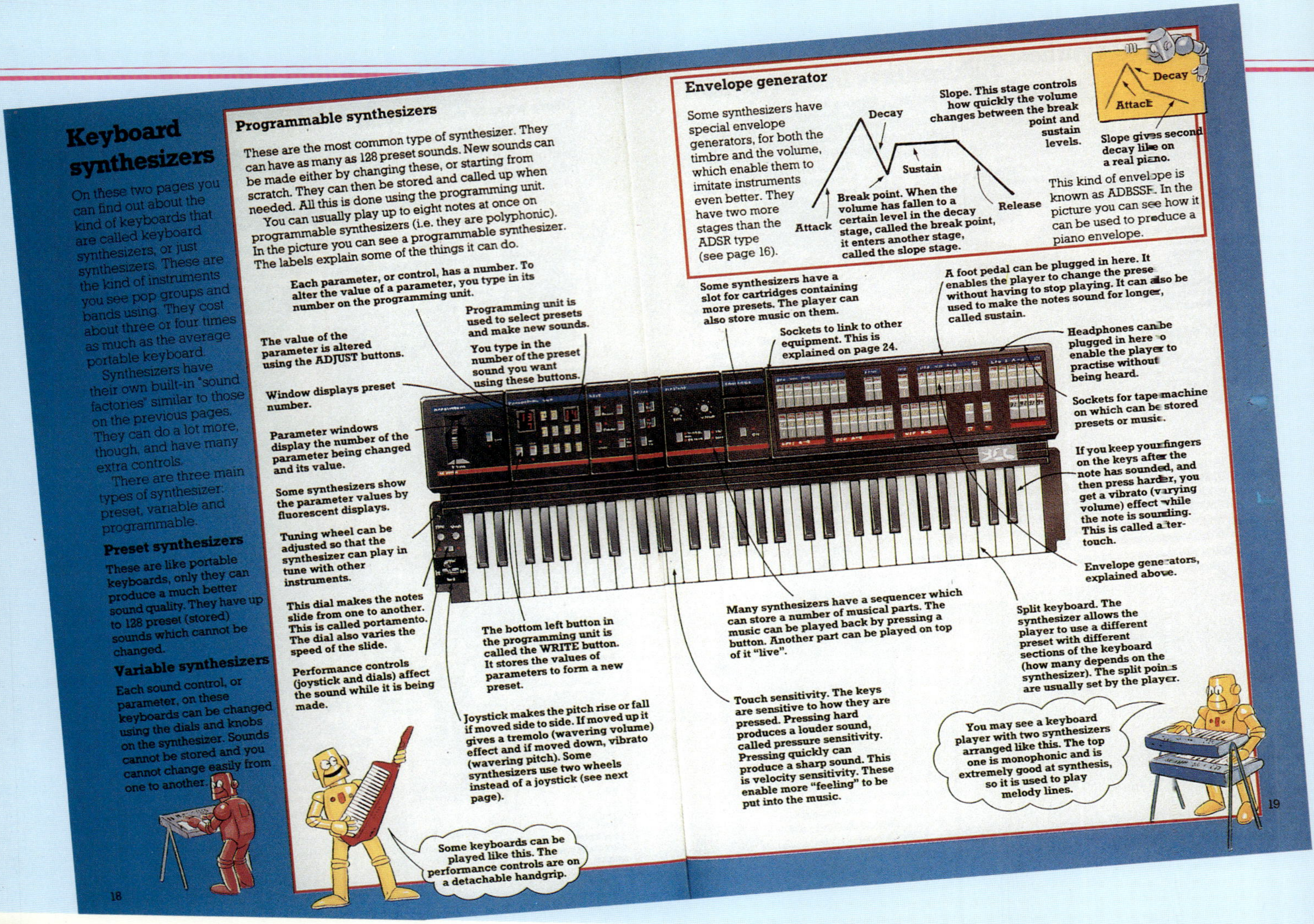

# Keyboard synthesizers

On these two pages you can find out about the kind of keyboards that are called keyboard synthesizers, or just synthesizers. These are the kind of instruments you see pop groups and bands using. They cost about three or four times as much as the average portable keyboard.

Synthesizers have their own built-in "sound factories" similar to those on the previous pages. They can do a lot more, though, and have many extra controls.

There are three main types of synthesizer: preset, variable and programmable.

## Preset synthesizers

These are like portable keyboards, only they can produce a much better sound quality. They have up to 128 preset (stored) sounds which cannot be changed.

## Variable synthesizers

Each sound control, or parameter, on these keyboards can be changed using the dials and knobs on the synthesizer. Sounds cannot be stored and you cannot change easily from one to another.

## Programmable synthesizers

These are the most common type of synthesizer. They can have as many as 128 preset sounds. New sounds can be made either by changing these, or starting from scratch. They can then be stored and called up when needed. All this is done using the programming unit.

You can usually play up to eight notes at once on programmable synthesizers (i.e. they are polyphonic). In the picture you can see a programmable synthesizer. The labels explain some of the things it can do.



18

## Envelope generator

Some synthesizers have special envelope generators, for both the timbre and the volume, which enable them to imitate instruments even better. They have two more stages than the ADSR type (see page 16).



This kind of envelope is known as ADBSSR. In the picture you can see how it can be used to produce a piano envelope.



19

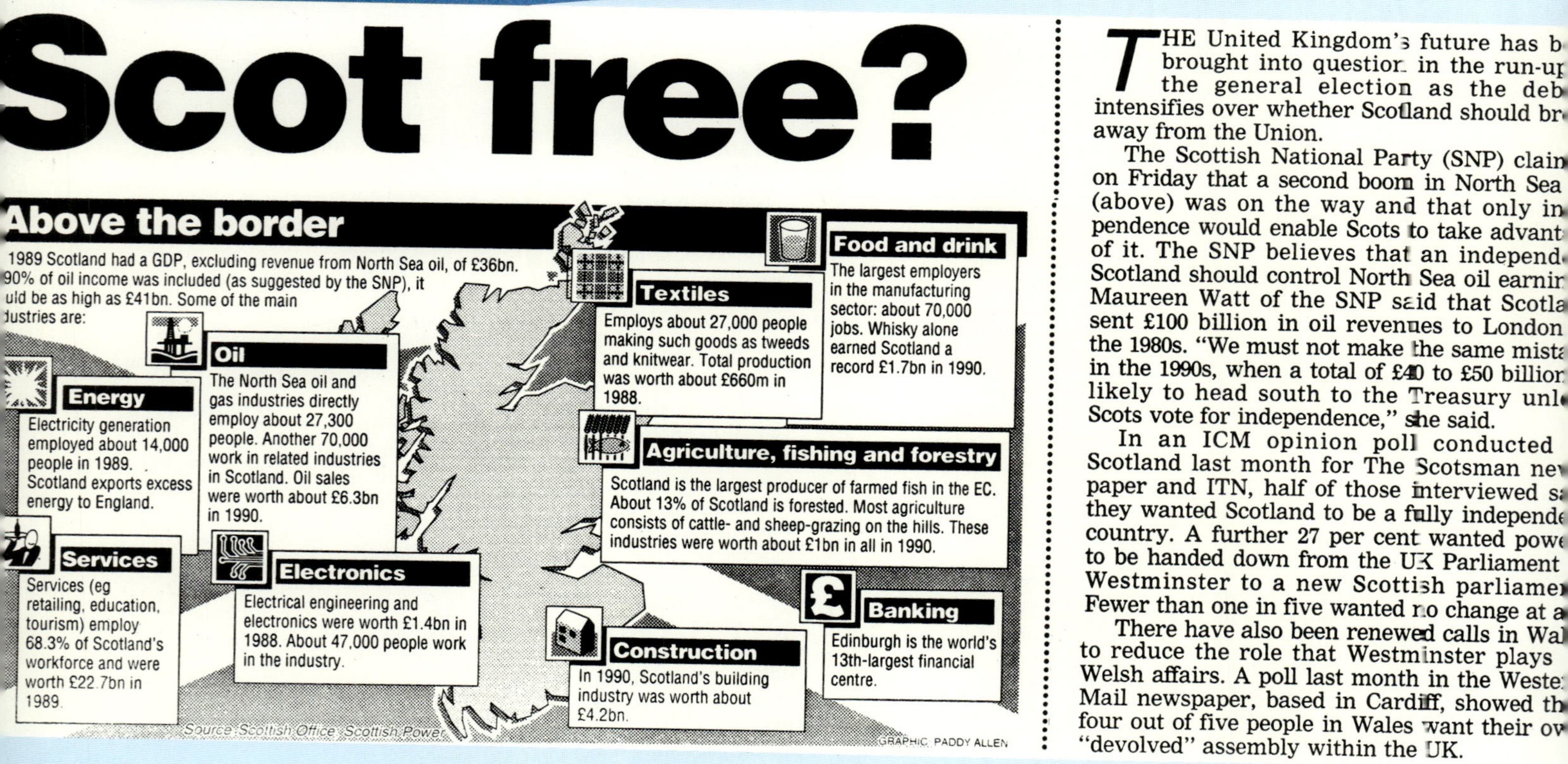

# Scot free?

## Above the border

1989 Scotland had a GDP, excluding revenue from North Sea oil, of £36bn. 90% of oil income was included (as suggested by the SNP), it uld be as high as £41bn. Some of the main dustries are:



THE United Kingdom's future has b brought into question in the run-up the general election as the deb intensifies over whether Scotland should br away from the Union.

The Scottish National Party (SNP) clain on Friday that a second boom in North Sea (above) was on the way and that only in pendence would enable Scots to take advant of it. The SNP believes that an independ Scotland should control North Sea oil earnin Maureen Watt of the SNP said that Scotla sent £100 billion in oil revenues to London the 1980s. "We must not make the same mista in the 1990s, when a total of £40 to £50 billion likely to head south to the Treasury unl Scots vote for independence," she said.

In an ICM opinion poll conducted Scotland last month for The Scotsman ne paper and ITN, half of those interviewed sa they wanted Scotland to be a fully independe country. A further 27 per cent wanted powe to be handed down from the UK Parliament Westminster to a new Scottish parliamen Fewer than one in five wanted no change at a

There have also been renewed calls in Wal to reduce the role that Westminster plays Welsh affairs. A poll last month in the Weste Mail newspaper, based in Cardiff, showed th four out of five people in Wales want their ov "devolved" assembly within the UK.

# Welcome to the Trust

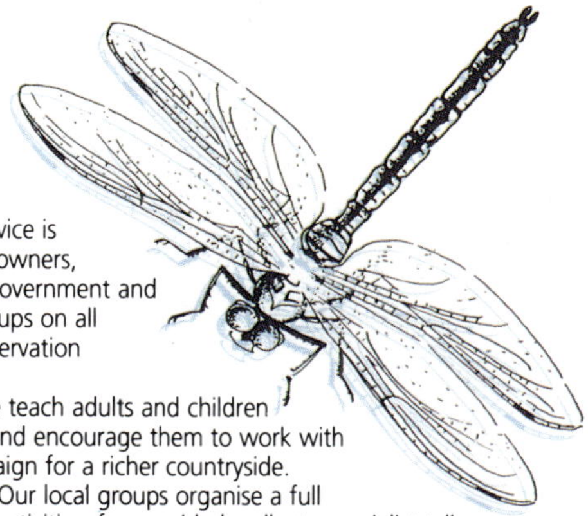

The Bedfordshire and Cambridgeshire Wildlife Trust was formed from two well established county trusts and is a member of the Royal Society for Nature Conservation Wildlife Trust's Partnership, the largest voluntary organisation in the UK concerned with all aspects of wildlife protection.
We support RSNC in their campaigns on national issues, particularly those that affect your local environment.
The Trust's concern is for wildlife of all types – animals, birds, reptiles, amphibians, fish, insects, plants and flowers.
We aim to protect them from pressures they cannot themselves resist. By joining The Trust you and your family can make an active contribution to conserving your local environment and help secure it for future generations.

**Our work**

***Conservation management:*** We manage over 90 nature reserves where wildlife is allowed to flourish and is protected forever against destruction and where members are free to visit.
***Campaigning:*** We care about the wider countryside too, campaigning to safeguard areas of special interest.
The Trust screens all local planning applications and, where we perceive a threat to wildlife, we fight to save the site.

***Advisory service:***
An advisory service is offered to landowners, farmers, local government and community groups on all aspects of conservation management.
***Education:*** We teach adults and children about wildlife and encourage them to work with us in our campaign for a richer countryside.
***Local groups:*** Our local groups organise a full programme of activities, from guided walks to specialist talks.
***WATCH:*** Through our WATCH groups, we help schools and youth groups take an interest in nature and supply them with back-up support and literature; we also run numerous adult courses and lectures of our own on wildlife and environmental issues.

Membership is fun – but with a serious purpose; and don't worry if you are inexp
hands to guide you c

**Your trust**

Just by joining The T
to conservation, but
also an interesting,
time. Whether you
are many other wa

- ***help with yo***
- ***join in a wor***
- ***alert us to p***
***environment***
- ***help with fu***
- ***help in one***
- ***lead childre***

As well as access
Trust's own new
*Natural World*, t

Supported by

E
N

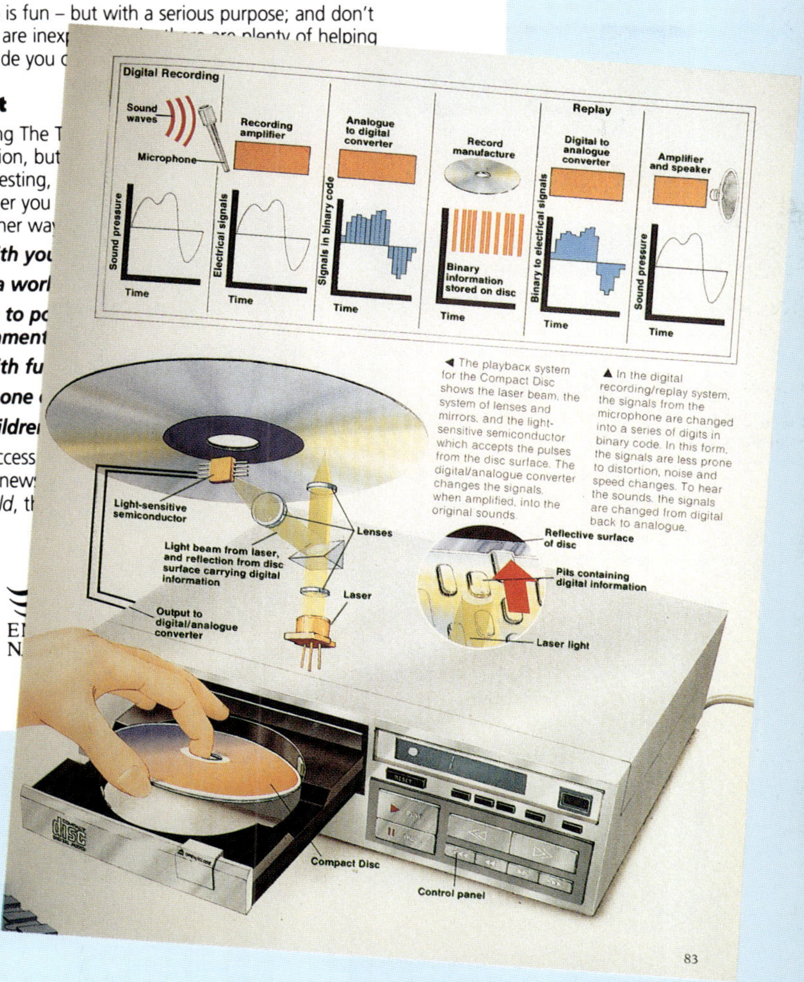


◀ The playback system for the Compact Disc shows the laser beam, the system of lenses and mirrors, and the light-sensitive semiconductor which accepts the pulses from the disc surface. The digital/analogue converter changes the signals, when amplified, into the original sounds.

▲ In the digital recording/replay system, the signals from the microphone are changed into a series of digits in binary code. In this form, the signals are less prone to distortion, noise and speed changes. To hear the sounds, the signals are changed from digital back to analogue.

83

## Netherlands

**Population: 14,443,000**
**Official language: Dutch**
**Currency: 1 gulden (guilder or florin, written: f1.) = 100 cents**

### Facts and information

The Netherlands became an independent constitutional monarchy in 1815, after a period of domination by France. At that time it also included what are now Belgium and Luxembourg. In an area of 15,900 square miles, the population density is over 1000 per square mile, the highest in Europe. The land is a large plain, half of which is below sea level and protected by dykes.

The Netherlands' climate is temperate – mild winters and wet summers. August is the month with the highest rainfall. Snow and ice are both common in winter.

The sovereign exercises power through a Council of Ministers, or Cabinet, with a Prime Minister at its head. Legislative power rests with the Parliament (known as the States General), in which there are two chambers. The First Chamber has 75 members, elected every four years by Provincial Legislative Councils. The Second Chamber has 50 members, elected every four years on a basis of proportional representation. There are about 820 municipalities governed by a burgomaster, aldermen and a council, who have the power to pass local regulations. The seat of government is in the Hague (population: 671,830), but the capital city is Amsterdam (998,310), which is the principal commercial and cultural centre. The second largest city is Rotterdam (568,000), which is the world's largest port.

Cheese and tulips are perhaps the best known products of Netherlands' fields. Both make a major contribution to the national economy. Since the war, 420,000 acres of land have been reclaimed from the sea, most of which is now being used as pasture land.

### Sport and culture

Football is the favourite sport. This is followed in popularity by gymnastics and water sports. Cycling is a way of life in this flat country. Skating is popular in winter. Weather permitting, the greatest annual skating event is the 'Eleven Towns' race held over 200 km.

**3** **Now, think about three additional ways of describing the features of informational writing. Pick one of the examples on pages 39 to 42 and study it more closely. What can you say about:**

- ☐ the *content* of the writing? What is the balance between facts (statements that most people would agree are scientifically, mathematically or generally agreed to be true) and opinions (statements that put forward one person's viewpoint or ideas)? Make a list of the main facts and anything which you think is comment or opinion.
- ☐ the *stylistic features* of the writing? Is the writing made up of long or short sentences? A mixture of both? What effect does this have on the way you read the information?
- ☐ the *layout* of the page? Is the page designed so that different kinds of information are grouped together? How are you shown that specific information is important? In what ways are details highlighted?

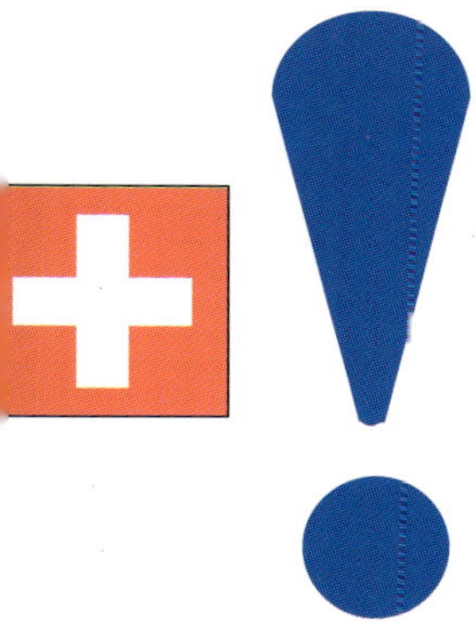

## IMAGES AND FIGURES

One thing you may have noticed in studying these examples of informational writing is the way that pictures and diagrams are often used to present information more clearly. These illustrations show some other ways in which information is presented, linking words and pictures.

| INFORMATIONAL WRITING | NOTES | EXAMPLES |
| --- | --- | --- |
| **Subject**<br>What is the writing about – people, things, ideas? | | |
| **Purpose**<br>What is the writer's aim or goal? How can you tell what it is? | | |
| **Audience**<br>Who is the writing for? What kind of relationship is there between the writer and the reader(s)? Friendly? Polite? Formal? | | |
| **Organisation**<br>How is the writing ordered and structured? What makes it hold together? | | |
| **Tense**<br>What tenses are used? Present? Future? Past? | | |
| **Other features**<br>What do the vocabulary and grammar of the writing reveal about it? Does the way that the page is laid out add to the effect? | | |

**4** **Find two or three more pieces of writing from books and magazines. Make a copy of the chart above on a larger sheet of paper and see how far you can describe each piece of writing by referring to the five writing features listed. Write brief notes and, if it is helpful, give examples from the extracts to support what you say.**

**5** **Now write one of the following. Use what you have learned about informational writing to make your writing more effective. Refer to the factfile on this page and be prepared to undertake some research before you start to write.**

- ☐ An account of a historical event which you have recently studied or investigated which could be included in a history book for 12 to 14 year-olds.
- ☐ A short guide to your local area which youth hostelers or caravaners would find helpful.
- ☐ The opening section of a guide for new students which gives helpful information about your school.
- ☐ A poster for display in your school as part of an anti-litter campaign.

## FACTFILE 4 — WRITING TO INFORM

When you want to present information remember that:

- the factual information about a subject is the *focus* for the writing
- the *purpose* of the writing is to *inform* people
- your *audience* can be anyone who is seeking these facts or pieces of information
- related pieces of information should be grouped together to help the reader
- you should normally use the present tense to give information which is true or correct at the time you are writing and the past tense for historical information
- informational writing can take many forms. Think carefully about the form you decide to use and whether it is the best way to convey your message.

# SETTING OUT

## POSTERS AND LEAFLETS

**A leaflet or a poster has first of all to catch a reader's eye. It must make the reader stop and look, so it needs a clear message. A good leaflet goes on to hold the reader's attention so that they read the small print and the details as well as the headline. When you are asked to design either a poster or a leaflet, think about the following points:**

### *1 THE MESSAGE*

What exactly do you want to say? What is the most important part of your message? Suppose you are selling second-hand books in the school hall on a particular date. Many people would make the date and place the most important part of the message rather than focusing on the fact that this is a book sale.

### *2 MAKE IT STAND OUT*

You can make readers notice your message in three ways:

- the size of the print,
- where it goes on your sheet,
- the words you use.

These have to be combined in an effective leaflet. 'LARGE SALE OF BOOKS' will not be very effective wherever it goes on the page, but 'THE CHEAPEST BOOKS IN TOWN' or 'BOOK BARGAINS GALORE' probably will.

### *3 THINK ABOUT INFORMATION*

Organise what you want to say into groups of related information. Here, the important information could concern the number and type of books, the place and the opening times. Then your information could finish with an encouraging summing up – DON'T MISS IT . . .

### *4 THINK ABOUT LAYOUT*

Set the information out on the page in a sensible sequence to match what goes on in the reader's head. What's this? A book sale. Are they the sort of books I'm interested in? Yes. When is it? Next Thursday. What time? All day. Don't miss it? I won't! Use boxes and different shapes for the writing to catch your reader's eye. Graphics which use the idea of books could help as well.

### *5 THINK ABOUT LANGUAGE*

As you revise the words of a poster or leaflet, think about being persuasive as well as informative. Check you are not using too many words. Keep your sentences short and the grammar and vocabulary simple. Look at each phrase in turn and check that it is giving the right message to a reader.

# NEUTRALITY AND BIAS

Informational writing involves the location and selection of factual information, which is then presented for a reader. As you have read the extracts featured on these pages, you may not have considered that their writers made decisions about what to include and what to leave out. When you wrote information, you did exactly the same thing.

However, it is possible to present information in ways which communicate quite different messages to a reader by the choice of what is included or left out. Writing which is selective about what it includes may be *biased* or one-sided in the information it presents. It may present the writer's view or the viewpoint of the organisation they work for. Although it contains facts, it may not give a *true* picture. Some people would even argue that all informational writing is biased because it *selects* information and *orders* it in particular ways.

**6** **Study the information opposite about a famous and controversial rock group who are about to make a comeback. Imagine that you work in the publicity department of Armada Records. Use the details to prepare a promotional sheet (about 500 words in length) which can be sent to newspapers and music journalists. Use the information to give a favourable view of the group.**

# THRILL MACHINE

## FOUNDED: 1983

MEMBERS: John Eadon (vocals), John Bowie (bass guitar), Steve Beale (drums), Harvey Robertson (rhythm guitar).

**March 1984** First release, 'I love your stuff', reaches no. 26 in BBC charts. John Bowie changes his name to Sid Damage.

**June 1984** Marquee Club, Manchester sells out all tickets for band performance. Group win *Music World* poll as Best New Band.

**July 1984** Band performance in Bolton leads to violence and hall seriously damaged. Promoter blames band for obscene lyrics and for inciting the audience.

**November 1984** Eadon swears during television interview. TV company switchboard jammed with callers. 'Damned Bad Show' LP released in Britain. Attacked for obscene lyrics. Defended by Bishop of Hull who points out that many young people sympathise with the group and their disenchantment with contemporary society. LP reaches no. 2 in LP charts.

**December 1984** Next single taken from LP – 'Dropped gear' – goes straight to no. 1 in British charts. Band's first release in US. Attacked as being about drugs but group say it is just a rock song.

US tour begins. Mixed reactions to group: 'Live anger and youthful venom' – *Rolling Stone* magazine; 'An awful cacophony of sound' – *Billboard* magazine.

**March 1985** Group 'trash' hotel suite in Denver. Arrested by local police. Charged with possession of drugs and heavily fined. Group claim they are innocent but remainder of tour is cancelled.

**April 1985** Steve Beale leaves group after allegations of drug taking and public quarrel with Sid Damage. Begins legal action against group for share of profits from last LP. Replaced by Lennie Wilson, previously with Eric Clapton backing group and respected guitarist.

**January 1986** 'City Dungeon' LP released. Reviewed as more accomplished than earlier work although some critics suggest it lacks the energy and bite of that material. Reaches no. 23 in LP charts by Easter.

**December 1986** Sid Damage on tabloid front pages after Christmas drinking sessions lead to spell at Betty Ford Clinic in USA for alcohol detoxification.

**March 1987** Eadon killed in car crash on M25. Postmortem shows evidence of alcohol and amphetamine drugs in bloodstream. Funeral attended by many fans.

**April 1988** Band announce they are splitting up. Sid Damage marries model Sylvie Kristel who has had his child.

**August 1990** Lennie Wilson and Harvey Robertson start touring together as 'Mighty H'. 'Thrill Machine Greatest Hits' LP with tracks from both albums flops.

**January 1991** 'Mighty H' have top five hit with 'I'm bad' and continue touring the club circuit. Follow up, 'Black Mother', is a smaller hit.

**Last year** Sid and Sylvie Kristel split up. Sid moves to USA and takes part in MTV anti-drug commercial with Michael Jackson and Whitney Houston.

**Three months ago** 'I love your stuff' used as backing track for advertisement for ICE jeans. Record re-released by Armada Records and goes straight to no. 1 for four weeks.

**Now** Armada Records re-sign group. Steve Beale comes back to group after working as a record producer in Los Angeles.

**7** **Now, imagine you work for *ZAP*, the newest and liveliest magazine about music. *ZAP* has an editorial policy of supporting young bands. Write a critical article about the re-launch of the band using the same set of information to give a *different* picture of 'Thrill Machine'. Give your article a title and make it about 400 words long.**

**8** In small groups, share out and study all the samples of informational writing collected by the class. Decide which ones, if any, are *biased* (putting forward a particular message as they give information). Then say which are mostly *neutral* or *objective* – presenting the information and leaving you, the reader, to make up your own mind. Report back as groups to the class and see how far you agree.

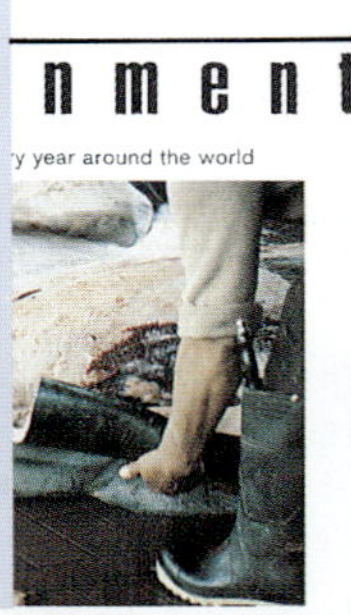

**Dolphin Friends**

The legacy of the 20th Century will include a damning record of extermination of the world's dolphins, porpoises and small whales, unless we act now to ensure their survival.

In just 3 years over 70% of one species - the Dall's porpoise - have been killed off the coast of Japan. Between 1979-89 21,000 pilot whales and dolphins were killed in the Faroe Islands. Modern fishing techniques, such as driftnets - the so called "Walls of Death"- are wiping out whole populations. Hundreds of thousands of dolphins are needlessly killed in this way every year.

EIA has campaigned to end this killing for over 6 years. Our **DOLPHIN FRIENDS** campaign was launched in 1990 to focus world attention on the problem. Dolphin Friends intends to save dolphins, porpoises and small whales by forcing the International Whaling commission (**IWC**) to regulate the killing.

In 1990 EIA achieved an historic breakthrough at the IWC, establishing a precedent for the protection of all small whales, porpoises and dolphins. 5,000 Dall's porpoises were immediately saved.

EIA will continue to expose the countries which oppose international protection. EIA will be investigating kills around the world. We are determined that these gentle and intelligent animals are given protection. But we need your support.

*"EIA are the cutting edge of environmental conservation and action. I can't think of any group more worthy of support".* HEATHCOTE WILLIAMS

**CONSUMER GUIDE**
**BY THE OBSERVER AND THE WOMEN'S ENVIRONMENTAL NETWORK**

- Buy recycled stationery, cards and wrapping paper
- Buy 100 per cent recycled, non-chlorine bleached toilet paper
- Use cotton nankies or (if you must) recycled tissues
- Use cloths instead of paper kitchen rolls
- Avoid paper bags (take your own reusable shopping bag) and overpackaged goods
- Recycle paper and reuse envelopes
- Encourage your office to buy recycled paper and recycle waste

**9** As you will have realised, informational writing comes in many closely related forms. Collect together your own selection of three pieces of informational writing taken from your own work in school. Write a commentary on what you have included and why. Try to show how the features of the writing enabled you to identify it as 'informational' and say how it might be improved.

## REWIND

- When you are asked to present information, think hard about the type of writing which is required. Then, decide how to group and organise your material before you begin to write. Make a plan to help you do this.
- As you write information, think where you might use the layout, graphics, diagrams or illustrations to make what you say clearer for your reader.
- As you revise, make sure your information is true. Check that your spelling of key words is correct and that numbers and dates are accurate.

# What I think

## OPINION AND PERSUASION

There are some subjects which always arouse strong feelings one way or the other every time they are discussed.

**1** **You will probably have an opinion about all of the slogans shown below and your own views as to whether or not you agree with them. Pick two or three of them and share your responses with your group.**

# VARIETIES OF TALK

When you talk, you may simply put forward your own view. However, as the talk develops into a discussion or possibly an argument, you may use your opinions to persuade other people to agree with you. When you are attempting to persuade someone to change their mind and agree with your views, then you will have to give reasons or examples to back up what you say.

In speaking and listening, the presentation of a point of view or an opinion takes many different forms. It might be a structured school debate where two sides take turns to present arguments. It could be a conversation where the people taking part agree with one another and the views expressed support each other. It could be an angry confrontation in a workplace about changed conditions or wages. Or it could be a class discussion where students give their views about a short story they have read.

As speakers, most people recognise the form of communication they are taking part in without consciously thinking about it. However, it can happen that the participants in a situation see it differently and may misunderstand the kind of communication which is taking place. For example, a customer taking faulty goods back to a shop may get very angry because, for them, a faulty compact disc or a split in a pair of new shoes seems very irritating. For the shopworker, the event is quite natural and their apparent lack of interest can enrage the customer. In this kind of spoken communication it is the mismatch in how the participants view it which leads to the argument.

In writing, there can also be a mismatching between what you want to say and the form you use. It is important to remember that choosing the best form for your writing will make you a more successful communicator. In school, you will often be asked to give your views in writing. You might be asked to:

At other times, you may be asked to give your own views as the conclusion to a set task, or you may want to give them at the end of a piece of writing of your own.

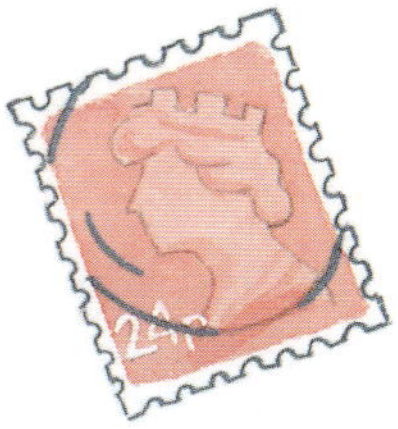

# VIEWPOINT 1

## *Letters*

One of the most common ways of giving your opinion in writing is in the form of a letter. The letters on pages 52–54 come from a range of sources and concern a wide variety of subjects.

**A**

12 MILTON KEYNES HERALD

### LETTERS TO THE EDITOR

DEAR SIR,
Ben Rood's letter last week misunderstands a vital point about roadside safety checks by the police and the possibility that they may then decide to breath test drivers.

The purpose of breath testing is to deter; it will only be successful when no driver has a blood alcohol level above the legal limit.

At present, drivers are very rarely stopped on the road; anyone who travels regularly sees examples of all kinds of bad driving by drivers who may or may not be over the limit for alcohol.

The traffic police do a good job. We need more of them, not fewer and they need to be better equipped. Otherwise, there will continue to be over 5000 deaths each year on Britain's roads.

JACK BIGLEY

**B**

**Dear 'Just 15',**

**I would like to reply to the letter from Laurence Doe published in your December magazine complaining about the recent pictures which have been shown of Madonna smoking.**

**Why, Laurence Doe, do you disagree with 'Just 15' printing these pictures as well as anti-smoking advertisements? Neither influence the readers of the magazine. The anti-smoking pictures only try to help people give up smoking and there's nowhere that Madonna says you must smoke because you're a fan of hers. She smokes because she wants to. It may be disgusting, smelly and could cause lung cancer but that's not the point.**

***Yours, Aleese Davies***

**C**

Dear Annette,

I was sorry to hear that you and Tomaso have broken off your engagement. Although you are probably very upset, I think that in the long run you will realise that it is for the best. It is hard to sustain a relationship over such a great distance and to really get to know someone, and I feel that you should neither of you be feeling guilty or upset about what has happened.

I believe that you should look upon the past two years as an enjoyable time when you learnt something about yourself on the road to adulthood.

Your loving aunt, Jessica.

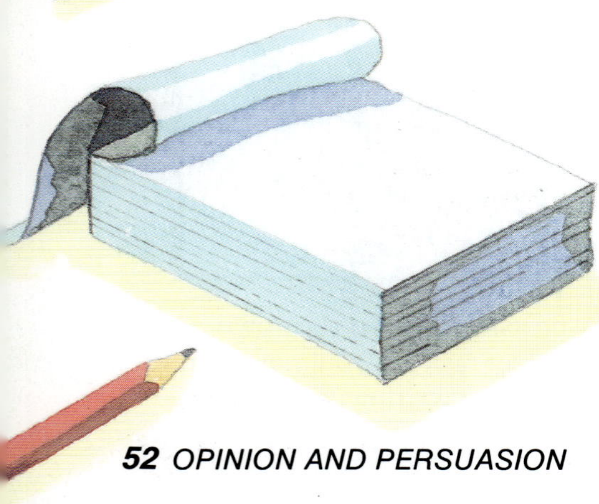

D

## BZ Magazine

## Letters

Dear Editor,

So your 'Ins and Outs' section says that pop stars over 35 will be unspeakable this year! This has made me realise just how commercialised the music industry has become, that only the young stars are accepted and, worse still, that magazines and newspapers continue to influence people into believing that these stereotyped, conveyor belt one-hit wonders make pleasurable music. Surely the music that bands produce is more important than their age or image.

If someone makes good music that is varied and interesting they should be regarded as talented and 'in' however old or young, fat or thin, tall or small. We need to get our priorities right. After all, even legends like Prince and Madonna are approaching the dreaded '35'.

*Yours faithfully*
*Sharon Smith (Leicester)*

E

Dear 'Evening News' Editor

We have heard much talk about the financial problems which beset zoos today, but what about the animals in them? The real question that must be considered is what to do with these animals once their 'homes' have been taken from them. Will they be re-housed elsewhere or, as seems more likely, be killed because the cost of finding new homes is too great?

In my view, the debate about the future of London Zoo needs to concentrate less on the problem of funding and more on the rights of the animals housed there and now under sentence of death.

**F**

The Rt Hon Eric Smith MP

House of Commons

Dear Mr Smith,

I am writing to you as my Member of Parliament to urge you to support the dog licensing bill which is currently being discussed in Parliament.

As a young child, I was severely bitten by a stray dog and still am very frightened of any unsupervised dog in the street. I think that dog owners should be quite happy to pay a small fee to have their dogs properly tagged and licensed to give people in the street a little peace of mind.

Yours sincerely,

Jason Barnes

**2** **With a partner, decide on the focus, purpose and audience for each one of the letters A–F. Make a chart like the one below to record your ideas. Then, join with another pair and exchange views. How far do you agree?**

| LETTER | FOCUS<br>the writer?<br>the reader?<br>the content? | PURPOSE<br>to inform?<br>to persuade?<br>to explain?<br>more than one of these? | AUDIENCE<br>one person?<br>a group?<br>someone else? |
|---|---|---|---|
| **A** | | | |
| **B** | | | |
| **C** | | | |
| **D** | | | |
| **E** | | | |
| **F** | | | |

Below is a reply to letter **A** (page 52). See how Ben Rood puts his opinions forward here. The notes show how the focus, purpose and audience for the writing are revealed in its language characteristics.

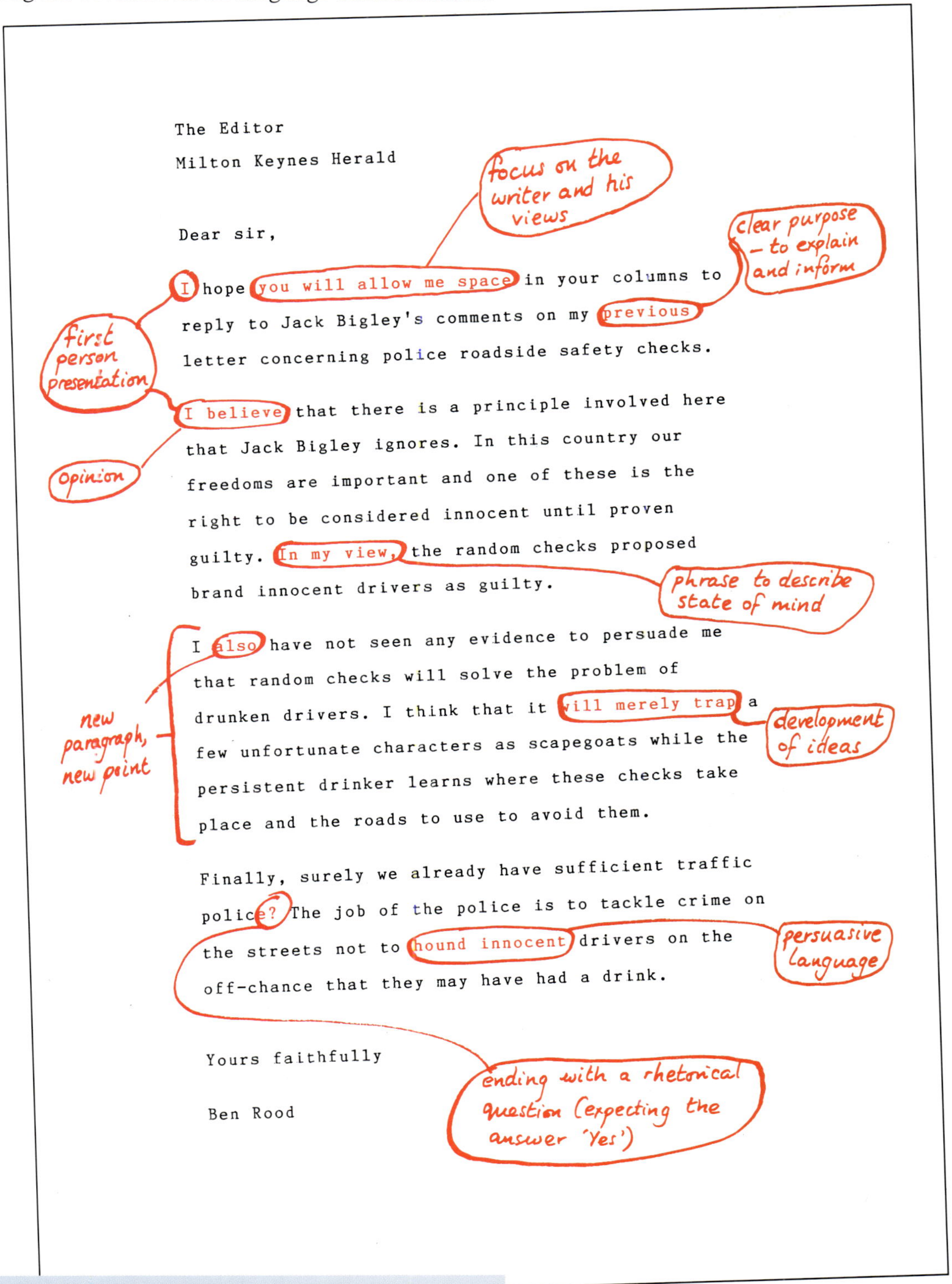

The Editor

Milton Keynes Herald

Dear sir,

I hope you will allow me space in your columns to reply to Jack Bigley's comments on my previous letter concerning police roadside safety checks.

I believe that there is a principle involved here that Jack Bigley ignores. In this country our freedoms are important and one of these is the right to be considered innocent until proven guilty. In my view, the random checks proposed brand innocent drivers as guilty.

I also have not seen any evidence to persuade me that random checks will solve the problem of drunken drivers. I think that it will merely trap a few unfortunate characters as scapegoats while the persistent drinker learns where these checks take place and the roads to use to avoid them.

Finally, surely we already have sufficient traffic police? The job of the police is to tackle crime on the streets not to hound innocent drivers on the off-chance that they may have had a drink.

Yours faithfully

Ben Rood



**3** **Pick out another letter from pages 52–54 for yourself and write your own reply to it, or your contribution to the argument it concerns.**

# SETTING OUT A LETTER

Setting out a letter is not hard. The first rule is to be consistent in the way you set out a letter and in how you punctuate it. The second is to use paragraphing to break up what you say into easy sections for a reader to follow.

For informal letters there are few rules. Your address is usually written in the top right-hand corner of the page with the date underneath. A line below, and on the left-hand side of the page, start your letter. Make sure you paragraph it to separate the things you want to say. End it politely. If you are not sure what to end with put 'Yours sincerely,' with your name underneath, written in your normal handwriting.

There are several acceptable ways of setting out a more formal letter, but the following hints suggest one way to make your finished product read better and look well presented.

65 Morgan's Hill
Taunton
Somerset
TA5 7UP

28 March

Dear Kerry

How are you? Just a quick note to say it was good to see you again the other day. You know, we should keep in touch. How about a letter from you? There's also a marvellous invention, you know – the telephone. It's easy to use and not too expensive.

Didn't ask if you had seen or heard from Jeremy lately. Last time I saw him was on 'EastEnders' – he was driving a taxi. Fame at last!

Keep in touch.

Yours sincerely, Susie

**1**

In a formal letter (i.e. a letter to someone you do not know personally or who you are writing to in an official way), include your address at the top of the letter on the left-hand side. Leave a margin (the left-hand margin). Underneath, put the date and the name, and/or position (job) and address of the person you are writing to. Punctuate these in a consistent way. Many writers would not put any punctuation marks at the line ends in the names or addresses here.

**3**

Leave a line and start writing your letter from the left-hand margin. Some writers 'indent' their letters so that they begin a little way across the page and under the name of the person they are writing to. If you do that for one paragraph, you should do it for all of them. Make each point in a separate paragraph. Do not worry if your paragraphs are very short.

**2**

If you know the name of the person you are writing to begin the letter 'Dear Mrs —', or 'Dear Mr —'; if you only know them by their position – Editor, Chief Personnel Officer or whatever – begin the letter, 'Dear Sir'. Only use 'Dear Madam' if you know that you are writing to a woman. DO NOT use 'Dear sir or madam'.

**4**

At the end of your letter put 'Yours sincerely' if you have used the person's name at the start and 'Yours faithfully' if you have used 'Dear Sir' or 'Dear Madam'. Put your name, written in your normal handwriting, underneath.

# VIEWPOINT 2

*Using evidence*

In any writing where you give your opinion, you will often find yourself wanting to make quite complex points which draw on a range of evidence and resources. The extracts on this and the next page are all concerned with the plight of young homeless people. In the past ten years there has been a noticeable increase in the numbers of people begging on the streets. To stop someone and ask for money is a crime but it is not illegal to sit by the side of a road, or on a railway station concourse, with a sign which does not actually ask for cash. Read the extracts through carefully before using them to give your own views.

Kevin arrived at Euston Station from his native Liverpool and stayed there. At 18 he's the oldest and most articulate. He also earns the bulk of the group's money by begging in the Euston underground.

He is embarrassed about begging. He can't look the public in the eye but sits scrunched up with his cap pulled down holding a "begging board" – a piece of cardboard saying "homeless and hungry". It is, generally, very lucrative.

"I now it's a bit of a con what we do," he says, "but we have to beg to survive. It's the only way we can live." He reckons to earn anything up to £200 a day for the group if he catches both rush hours and once made a record £34 in 15 minutes.

There are more than sufficient Employment Training places in all parts of the country for all who want them – well over 100,000. Some young people find their own training places, but those who want a place should keep in regular touch with their local careers office. If, for any reason, a suitable place is not immediately available, the careers office can and does get in touch with our local Training Agency Office who have the authority and resources to provide more places. Training provides a sound foundation of increasing importance for the future working lives of young people and the overwhelming majority of those who go on such courses find them a worthwhile way to make the bridge from school to work.

In April 1988 Supplementary Benefit was replaced by Income Support. Amounts payable as Income Support vary by age. In 1992 the rates were:

| | |
|---|---|
| 18–24 | £33.60 a week |
| over 25 | £42.45 a week |

In September 1988 the age of entitlement to Income Support was raised to 18 years with the exception of cases of severe hardship.

"The stereotype might be that they are lazy and idle, but these kids are often more enterprising and less apathetic than those who stay behind . . . They've taken advice and got on their bikes. Their begging is short term, aimed at acquiring the cash to afford somewhere to live. Without an address, many employers will not look at a young job applicant so they remain trapped by their poverty."

Nick Hardwick *director of Centrepoint, a night shelter for homeless young people*

Darren: "From Manchester, London looked full of film stars walking around the West End . . . full of yuppies all rich and famous. But it ain't. In fact, London's full of tramps, homeless like me and if we stop begging we'll have to go back home and that's worse!"

"About 80 per cent of 16 to 18 year-olds live with a family, and they have seen a real increase in their benefits, so we are talking about a small minority of young people who are living independently. It must be emphasised that they receive maximum help with rent and rates."

Marcus had a troubled childhood and was taken into care at 15 and, by 17, had developed a gambling problem. He is unable to hold down a job and alternates between casual labour and unemployment. Before the April changes his state income was £52.40 a week which he spent on rent and rates (£22), food (£15), fuel (£5), fares (£5) and clothes, laundry and leisure (£5). After April, Marcus's income was reduced to £35.99 – but his expenses were unchanged. Begging at Victoria Station was one way to compensate for this.

**4** **Read the letter below which was sent to a London evening newspaper. Write a detailed reply to this letter giving your own views. You can support, oppose or correct anything the writer says but try to present your own point of view clearly. As you write:**

- *focus* on yourself, your opinions and your reactions to Mr Wilson's points;
- make the *purpose* of your writing to inform other people of your views or to persuade them to agree with you;
- imagine the *audience* for your letter to be readers of the newspaper, perhaps people who see the same things as Mr Wilson does on their journeys to work.

The Editor
'The Evening Telegraph'
Telegraph House
Ward Street, London E3

Dear Sir,

Once again my journey from station to office has been impeded by the beggars who congregate in and around Waterloo Station. Can anyone explain why there are more and more of these degenerates?

After all, the papers are crammed full of jobs in the city and firms are evidently desperate to recruit young, willing workers so why is this problem allowed to persist in our streets? I thought it was illegal for beggars to solicit in the street in this country and these children with their scrawled notice boards are doing just that.

We can all imagine where the money they make from innocent daytrippers and visitors goes to as well. To buy drink and drugs of course - what else? And how must tourists feel when their first sight of this country at the end of the Heathrow Line looks like some far eastern shanty town? It is time something was done.

Yours faithfully

M K Wilson

**5** **Write one of the following, choosing a subject from list A and choosing a form from list B.**

**A**
THE NEED FOR DOG LICENSING
FOX AND DEER HUNTING
CIGARETTE SMOKING BY YOUNG PEOPLE

**B**
A CLASS TALK
A NEWSPAPER EDITORIAL
A LETTER TO A MAGAZINE

## FACTFILE 5 OPINION WRITING

If you are asked to write opinion remember that:

- the *focus* of the writing is on you, the writer, and your views
- the *purpose* of the writing is to present those views and to share them with others
- the *audience* can be any number of people – from a single person to an unknown group. You do not need to know exactly who your audience is before you start to write.
- the writing must be organised around your ideas and opinions. It may help to make each idea a separate paragraph and to try to make a point in one sentence and then develop it with an example to show exactly what you mean.
- you will need to use the first person and verbs or phrases which describe a state of mind such as 'I think . . .', 'I believe . . .' and 'In my view . . .'.

# VIEWPOINT 3

## *Writing to persuade*

In writing your letter you may have seen how writing which expresses an opinion can also both inform and persuade. Putting forward an opinion invites other people to agree with what you say and, to that extent at least, an opinion is always persuasive. However, some writing sets out to persuade and convince the reader more deliberately.

The leaflets on these pages were produced by different organisations and 'pressure groups' in an attempt to change people's minds on particular issues. They are deliberately persuasive. What this means is that they set out to show a reader that they ought to do something, support a cause or take on a belief. The writing tries to convince the reader by its selection of information and reasons, and by an appeal to the reader's good sense or sympathies.

In Turkey a pregnant woman detainee is punched in the stomach by police officers. An elderly Indian woman is raped in front of her family by armed soldiers. A young girl is detained and sexually harassed by Moroccan governmental officials. In Syria a wife is tortured by interrogators to force her husband to "confess". A Sri Lankan mother is shot dead by soldiers because her son is suspected of political activities. A daughter is threatened with death by government forces in the Philippines, because she asks after her "disappeared" father.

Amnesty International's list of gross human rights violations against women around the world is endless. Neither the pregnant nor the elderly are protected.

**strong**

Many women are targeted because they are **strong** — because they are political activists, community organisers or because they persist in demanding that their rights and those of their relatives are respected. As more women reach out for equality and participation in the governance of their society, they become more visible within that society and so more likely to face repression.

**vulnerable**

Many women are also targeted because they are vulnerable — gender difference causes women to be perceived as easy targets for both physical and psychological abuse: young women who can easily be sexually abused; frightened mothers desperate to protect their children; pregnant women fearful for their unborn babies; women who can be used to get at male relatives; refugee women isolated in an alien environment at the mercy of authorities with the power to grant them necessary food or documentation.

*providing help to ... effects.*

*To help you spot drugs or evidence of their use we've pictured some of the things to look out for.*

**Amphetamines (Speed).** Commonly a white or brown powder but can be in pill or capsule form. Usually sniffed or injected. Makes people lively, giggly and over-alert, but depression and difficulty with sleep can follow. Heavy use can produce feelings of persecution.

**Cannabis, (Pot, Dope, Hash, Grass).** Hard brown resinous material or herbal mixture. Smoked in a reefer or pipe, sometimes with tobacco. Distinctive "herbal" smell. Users may appear "drunk" and talkative. Risk of accidents when intoxicated.

**Cocaine (Coke).** A white powder, commonly sniffed. Can be injected or sometimes smoked. Similar effects to amphetamines but more likely to lead to dependence.

**Heroin (Smack, Skag).** White or speckled brown powder. Usually heated on silver foil and fumes inhaled. Can be sniffed or injected. Produces initial alertness followed by drowsiness and "drunken" appearance. Overdose can produce unconsciousness. Regular, frequent use produces dependence. Abstinence in a regular user can result in physical withdrawal symptoms similar to flu.

**Magic Mushrooms.** Mushrooms eaten fresh or dried. Grow wild in the UK. Similar effects to Cannabis. Main risk arises from eating other poisonous mushrooms.

**Other Opioids (dikes, 118s).** May include red or white tablets or ampoules. Swallowed or injected. Same effects as heroin.

... mouth. Produces glazed eyes and sometimes over-excitement. Heavy use can produce acute confusion and ideas of persecution.

**Tranquillisers.** Prescribed tablets and capsules sometimes taken illegally for kicks. Similar effect to alcohol and increased effect when taken with alcohol.

**Injecting.** Many drugs can be injected. Risks are abscesses, infected veins, blood poisoning, hepatitis and AIDS virus infection.

**WHAT CAN BE THE DANGERS OF DRUGS?**

The main dangers are as follows:

- Having an accident while under their influence.
- Some drugs may depress or stop breathing.
- Accidental overdose can lead to unconsciousness or even death.
- Addiction or dependence, after regular use.

In addition to these dangers, drugs can also have nasty side effects.

They can bring on confusion and frightening hallucinations.

They can cause unbalanced emotions or more serious mental disorders.

First time heroin users are sometimes violently sick.

Regular users may become constipated and girls can miss their periods.

Later still, there may be more serious mental and physical deterioration.

And if a drug user starts to inject, infections leading to sores, abscesses, jaundice, blood poisoning and even AIDS virus infection may follow.

**6** **With a partner, look more closely at the leaflets. Try to identify:**

- ☐ the existing state of affairs which the writers want to change
- ☐ their arguments
- ☐ the kind of change they believe is possible
- ☐ their recommendations as to what the readers can do.

**Report your views back to the class.** Do you think that the effectiveness of the leaflets is related to how many of these things they do well?

7 Look back at the information on homelessness on pages 57 and 58 and the advice on poster writing on page 45. Below is the outline for a poster which is to be displayed at main railway stations. Its aim is to present information which will *persuade* teenagers not to run away to London. Using this layout, and the information, create your own poster. Remember that what you write has to make the reader think twice. It needs to be clear, direct and persuasive.

# LONDON ISN'T PAVED WITH GOLD!

**Under 18? Thinking of going to London on your own? Think again! Are you sure you know?**

★ **What it's really like . . .**

★ **Where you could end up . . .**

★ **What's best for you . . .**

**SO THINK AGAIN . . .**

As you planned and wrote your poster, you will have realised that you had to think hard about your reader and what they would notice if they saw it. That focus on the reader rather than yourself is a major difference between writing opinion and persuasion. The other major difference is that persuasive writing sets out to change someone's views and may use language in quite deliberate ways to make that happen. In the leaflet below, some of the ways this can be done are highlighted for you.

## FACTFILE 6 WRITING PERSUASIVELY

If you are asked to write persuasively remember that:

- the *focus* of the writing is on the reader and on your attempts to change their views;
- the *purpose* of the writing is to persuade the reader that the views expressed in the writing are correct or in their best interest;
- the *audience* can be any number of people – from a single person to an unknown group. Knowing who your audience is before you start to write helps you to target the writing specifically at particular people or groups.
- the writing must be organised in stages or in groups of ideas which the reader can follow and accept. It may also exaggerate or even distort the truth to give an added effect to what is described.
- you may need to use the second person ('you') and verbs or phrases which encourage, threaten or appeal to the reader. Phrases like 'you should', 'you ought' and 'you would' or which use 'if . . . then' constructions may be a feature of the writing.

## DON'T LET THEM RUIN YOUR LIFE . . .

Young people today are spoilt. Brought up with too much money, too much television and too much attention, they have become a rude and lazy rabble.

You have seen them hanging round in streets with their bikes and skateboards, smoking, writing on walls with spray paint and dropping sweet and gum wrappers wherever they go.

You know it's time to do something about this menace and bring back discipline, smart dress and respect. If you don't act now, then tomorrow may be too late. Would you like loutish youths to go on terrorising old people and stealing their valuables?

If not, act now. Join the *Campaign Against Young Hooligans* and see a change for the better now and a brighter tomorrow ahead.

# VIEWPOINT 4

*Longer writing assignments*

One problem writers have to face is in telling when they are being asked to give an opinion apart from the times when they are being asked to write persuasively.

**8** **Look at these writing tasks with a partner and decide whether they should be responded to as persuasion or opinion. Use the notions of focus, purpose and audience to help you decide. Share your findings with another pair. How far do you agree?**

**A** The late-night bus service to your home area has been suspended after a few people caused some trouble. Write a letter to your local councillor asking for the service to be restored.

**B** Too much snooker? Too little football? Few sports covered which interest women? Give your views on the present television coverage of sport.

**C** Write a letter which can be sent home from your school tutor group to parents, asking them to support your charity appeal for Cancer Research.

**D** If you had the chance, which country in the world would you like to visit on a three-month study and holiday tour?

**E** What 'rights' are animals entitled to?

F

Write a leaflet for display in primary schools about the dangers of solvent abuse.

G

In rainforest areas which is more important – the needs of the native populations or the conservation of the forests?

H

At what other periods in British history would you like to have been alive? Why?

I

How can people best be persuaded to change their behaviour in response to the threat from HIV infection and the Aids virus?

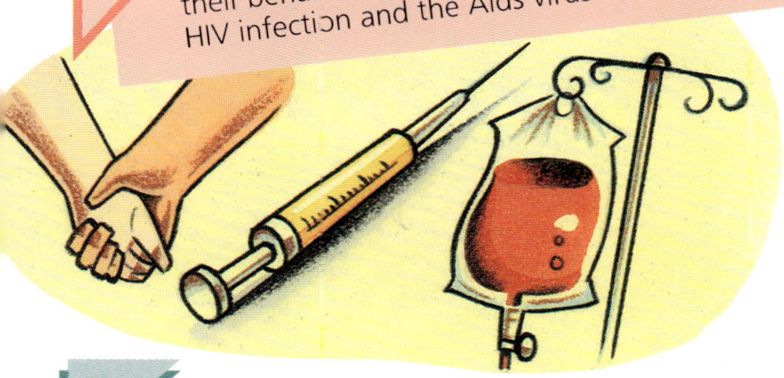

J

Poll tax, rates or local income tax? What kind of local taxation would you prefer to pay?

## *What's bugging you?*

**9 Look back to the start of this section on page 49 and the slogans there. Pick a subject you feel strongly about, research the evidence and put your own views down in a sustained piece of writing for your group to read. Use what you have found out about writing types to help you and think carefully about the focus of your writing.**

### REWIND

- When you approach a task which asks for your views or ideas, first decide whether you are being asked to write opinion or persuasion.
- In writing opinion make sure that the sequence of your ideas will allow a reader to follow what you want to say and understand the points you are making. Give your reasons as well as your views.
- As you write persuasively, remember that the changing of your reader's views is what you want most of all to achieve, so argue firmly and powerfully. Use appropriate sentence constructions and a colourful vocabulary to help you.

# 5

# What it's like

## DESCRIPTIVE WRITING

One of the most important ways in which people use language is to describe to one another their experiences and feelings. We take for granted our ability to communicate the quality of events and to say not only what happened to us but also to describe what it was like.

With friends you know well, this process is almost unconscious. You already share many of the same experiences and know the same places and people. However, you will probably recognise the feeling of coming back from somewhere – a holiday, a concert or a visit – and telling your friends about new people you have met and places you have visited. This section explores a writing type which builds up detailed descriptions and can evoke, or recreate for a reader, the impression of being somewhere else.

## Wish you were here!

The essential human feature which allows people to describe their own experiences and to share and appreciate other people's experiences is the *imagination*. Surprisingly little is known about how the human brain can take fragments of ideas, a few experiences and a handful of sensations and turn them into a complete scene.

**1** **With a partner, look at the pictures on these pages. Talk about what you can see in them and what they suggest to you. They show snapshots of scenes but you can use the visual clues in them to build up a surprisingly detailed description.**

# Lanzarote

Puerto del Carmen is the islands main resort



Lanzarote is the nearest of the Canaries to the coast of Africa, and it has even clearer skies and less rainfall than the other Canary Islands. All this makes it the perfect place for a holiday in the sun. What's more, island, it has barely been touched by the 20th century. The main attractions are basking upon mile after mile of uncrowded beaches and exploring the strange volcanic landscape. If you want something more active try snorkelling or other watersports. As for nightlife, there are a few discos, but the most popular way to spend the evenings is taking relaxed meals in local seafood restaurants, then enjoying good company in seafront bars. The smart, purpose-built resort of **Costa Teguise** continues to develop and increase in popularity thanks to its beach of fine, dark sand and excellent sports facilities including tennis, golf and windsurfing. Nightlife here is low-key with a selection of bars and a disco or two centred around the main hotel and apartment complexes. **Puerto del Carmen**, the island's main resort, is ideal for the young and lively or for families. It has grown up alongside a long curve of gently-sloping fine dark sand beach. Popular sports here include tennis, squash and waterskiing, plus excellent windsurfing conditions. A superb range of restaurants as well as bars and some discos help keep evenings varied and good fun. **Playa Blanca** provides a complete contrast. A quiet, relaxing resort, it is a former fishing village which has developed without losing its character. There's a small sandy beach, with more excellent beaches at nearby Papagayo, and a promenade with bars and restaurants.



Skytours

## *Sensory messages*

Choose one illustration to explore on your own. You need to be as quiet as possible for this and to concentrate hard so that all your attention is focused on the scene.

1 Start by jotting down what you can see in the picture. Note what people are doing and use adjectives to describe some of the things you can see.

2 So far you have used one sense – sight. Now take each of the other four senses in turn. Start by describing what you would hear if you were drawn into the scene you have chosen. Then think about smells, tastes and touch. You will notice that some things give off much stronger sensory messages than others. Often the most effective description is made up of a number of sensory impressions mixed together. Food cooking, a warm breeze and splashing in sea water are all examples of situations where all your senses are alerted.

3 Develop your description into a first draft. Only write on alternate lines. Try to organise the sensations you describe so that a reader will be drawn into, or led round, the scene. Use the present tense (as if you are looking at the scene now) to make your writing more involving for your readers and to make them feel as if they are present.

4 As you redraft, aim to add description with adjectives, adverbs and comparisons. Use the space you have left between the lines and expect the writing to increase in length as you extend your description.

5 Revise your writing and produce a final copy. Ask yourself whether the description you have written takes your reader 'inside' the scene. Check that you have done enough to suggest the sound of the scene you have described.

6 Form groups with people who chose the same scene and review your work. You will probably find that you all agree quite closely about which descriptions are the most effective. Think about why. Is it the selection of details or the range and quality of the descriptive words which influences you? Or is it the way the writer leads you, as a reader, into the scene?

## WHAT IS A DESCRIPTION?

Read this description of the Indian city of Delhi by Trevor Fishlock. Afterwards, talk with your partner about how the writer has managed to convey a sense of movement and colour into his description by appealing to all of the senses. Part of the description is highlighted to show some of the ways in which this is done.

8

# A Tale of Three Cities

THE FLEETING, savoured spring of the plains of northern India has almost passed and we shall soon be in the furnace, meek subjects of the sun. Along Delhi's broad boulevards the trees have suddenly greened and spread into parasols. The first of the season's water carts are being wheeled on the cracked and betel-stained pavements, the nation's cuspidor. A glass of chilled water is less than a halfpenny. In the old part of the city, where pungent spicy smells linger in the narrow secret streets, the traditional water sellers hump leaking goatskin bags on their backs and squirt water into little tin cups. Customers swill and toss coins into the sellers' marsupial pouches. There will soon be times when I shall envy the ice men: they strap large blocks of ice beneath their bicycle saddles with hairy string and know the pleasure of cool buttocks on roasting days.

The garden is bright with snapdragons, roses, dahlias, daisies, hibiscus and bougainvillea, flamboyant as a matador's cape. Bulbuls, with jaunty Robin Hood caps, red cheeks and red underwear are contesting the lime tree with sparrows. Mynahs have bursts of communal violence, or stride self-importantly up and down, shrieking like politicians in parliament. On the wall doves gaze into each other's eyes. Lizards are out scouting, signallers of summer. A little way off, an elephant proceeds on his lawful occasions with stately stride, the bell swinging beneath this middle donging like the call to evensong heard across a meadow.

Outside there is a dusty road, its edges swept by women forever bent over their stiff brushes in the attitude of Millet's gleaners. Cooks bicycle by with their shopping baskets, flitting bee-like from market to market, from meat to fish to fruit to cheese to vegetables, ordering chickens off to instant execution. Shopping can be a complex operation. There are no supermarkets; nor, one imagines, will there ever be, for they would be so much against the Indian grain of small and intimate family businesses and little shoulder-rubbing shops grouped together in like trades. Across the road is a maidan, the village green of this neighbourhood, surrounded on three sides by houses and tall trees. Some boys are playing cricket on it, and it is a serious affair, with the batsmen looking pukka in pads. I ought to move inside to avoid being brained by a six. There is an evocative smell of newly cut grass, which for me always means cricket. The maidan was cut this morning by a mower drawn by an ox, and now the beast is grazing up in one corner while the mower-wallah dozes under a tree.

There must be a dozen men in white dhotis slumbering in patches of shade, and out in the sun a group of women in red and green saris, servants and the wives of servants, sit in a circle with their small children, talking and laughing.

Strolling schoolgirls in white dresses, their shiny hair in thick plaits, lick ice cream cornets bought at the shop around the corner. That place is a magnet: every evening the little piazza in front of it is crowded with men, women and children sucking ice cream and popping sweet and sticky things into their mouths with dripping fingers. ~~It is a carefree congregation, lapping at the evening waterhole of sugar indulgence. Indians love sweets and the price of sugar is politically sensitive.~~ The children have white mouths and splashed shirts, the women have ~~desired~~ rolls of waistline fat which wobble as they chatter like jolly parrots. Fastened to their waists, and jingling in concert with the wobbling, are the keys to their houses, refrigerators, jewellery boxes, money drawers and whiskey cupboards. The men stand with their ice cream or plates of sweetmeats, talking about cricket or absent in reverie. They are oblivious to the confusion and jam they have caused in the road by their inconsiderate parking. Indians do not park: they arrive and stop – and what happens around them is someone else's problem. In the road there is rage, gesticulation and scratched bodywork, but in the piazza of sugary peace and closed ears it is of no concern as tongues lovingly carve ice cream cones into periwinkles.

// There is a group of men lolling on the maidan grass, wearing white uniform jackets, blue trousers, black boots and red caps, and around them lie drums, trumpets, horns, a sousaphone and bells. Crisp they are not: they are a wedding band and soon they will start up the tremendous blaring and crashing that accompanies a Hindu bridegroom as he processes to the meeting with his bride at the sacred fire. The groom's transport, a white horse with a red velvet saddle, is nearby, nibbling at the grass the ox mowed. In the road is the gaudy mobile bandstand, equipped with loudspeakers, which will be pushed along by sweating minions.

Some boys are flying kites and the upperworks of the trees are full of crashed ones. There are also forktailed kites of the feathered kind swinging in circles overhead. At their altitude they can see one of their food sources, the swimming pool at the large hotel down the road. Many an air stewardess, glistening at the poolside, has been astonished to see her club sandwich lifted from its plate by one of these insolent thieves, right under her Ambre Solaire'd nose.

130

adjectives

metaphor to describe how it attracts people like a magnet attracts metal

appeal to taste and touch

simile

sound of 'w' repeated for effect

appeal to sound and hearing

a list of items

START HERE

**2** **Make a copy of the chart below and use it to analyse the section of the writing outlined by noting down the different senses the writing appeals to.**

| SIGHT | HEARING | SMELL | TASTE | TOUCH |
| --- | --- | --- | --- | --- |
| | | | | |

**3** **Now, practise these descriptive skills within your group in one of the following ways:**

- ☐ Each bring in a picture, a photograph or an illustration from a newspaper or a magazine. Exchange them so that you use someone else's as the starting point for your writing. Write a description of what you see.
- ☐ Spend one lunchtime observing a crowded school entrance hall, cafeteria or playground. Write a description inspired by Trevor Fishlock's account.

# ALL IN THE MIND

It is quite possible to write descriptively about places you have never visited or are very unlikely to visit. Your imagination can put together old memories and associations to create a convincing picture even though you will probably find that it is impossible to remember or identify where all the images originated.

**THE SURFACE OF THE MOON**
**THE SOUTH POLE**
**THE CRATER OF A VOLCANO**

**With a partner, think hard about what your first impression of each of these places is like. Jot down words and ideas as they come to mind. Making and using a chart like the one on page 71 or a spider plan like the one opposite, may help you to note down the images and pictures which these places suggest to you.**

**Finally, pick one situation and write your own description as if you were there.** As you write like this, you will be bringing even more of yourself and your own background knowledge to the writing. This kind of descriptive writing, where you explore your own personal response as well as the setting, is sometimes called *reflection*. You could write this quite effectively in the form of a poem.

**The main difference between reflection and description is that if you make the scene into the focus for your writing then you will be writing description. But, if you focus more on your own responses as a writer, then you are likely to be writing reflection.**

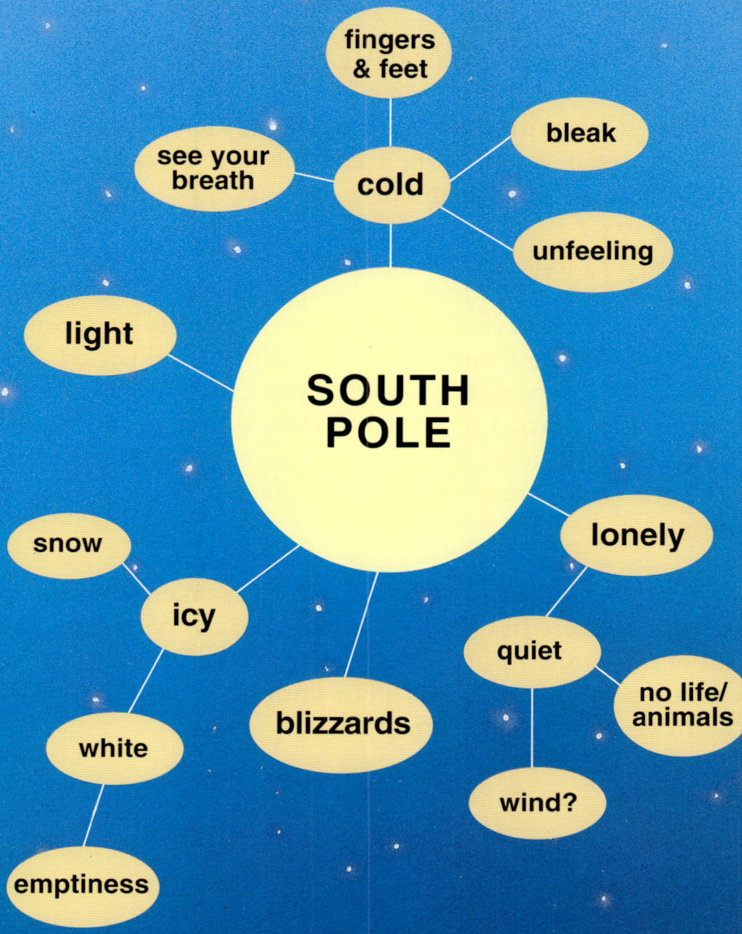


## FACTFILE 7 DESCRIPTION AND REFLECTION

If you are asked to write description or reflection remember that:

- for **description**, the *focus* of the writing is the subject being described; for **reflection**, it is the writer's responses as well which are important
- the *purpose* of both types of writing is to create an impression of a place, people or time which is as lifelike as possible
- the *audience* can be anyone or any group of people but thinking about them – and what they already know – may help to improve your writing
- the writing should be made up of a series of linked observations and images, or connected impressions. Try to make your words follow a viewer's eye across a scene.
- the writing should use adjectives, adverbs and comparisons to build up its descriptive effect. For reflection, there should be plenty of reference back to the writer and their feelings.

## BEING THERE – EMPATHIC WRITING

When you were writing reflectively you may have found it helped to imagine yourself as part of the scene you were describing – and to 'look around' the scene in your mind.

Sometimes in English lessons, you will be asked to do this and to imagine that you are a character in a novel or play. Or you could be asked to write a new scene or a different ending for it. In History, you could be asked to write as if you were living in a particular historical period. Whatever you do, you will be expected to use what you know of the novel or play, or what you have learned about that historical time to add detail to your writing and to make it authentic – as realistic as possible. Writing where you view a scene through the eyes of someone else is called *empathic* writing.

With a partner, read the extract below. It is taken from *Empty World* by John Christopher. In the story, Neil Miller has been left alone after the death of his family in an accident. Then a deadly plague wipes out almost the entire population. Neil is alone until he finds a deflated balloon with an address on. He goes there at once . . .

### THE PLAGUE

A sports car was standing outside, its relatively clean windscreen evidence of recent use. Neil parked behind it and climbed out into the hazy sunshine. He ought to have put a sign up outside his own house, he realised. For that matter, he should have thought of something like the balloons. The inhabitant of no. 34 was obviously more enterprising.

The front door was not locked. He opened it and stepped into the hall. He called out: "Hi, there! Anyone home?" There was no reply. He had a moment's disappointment but only that. At this time of day, he himself would have been more likely to be out than in. The stranger would have his own routine of walks and foraging.

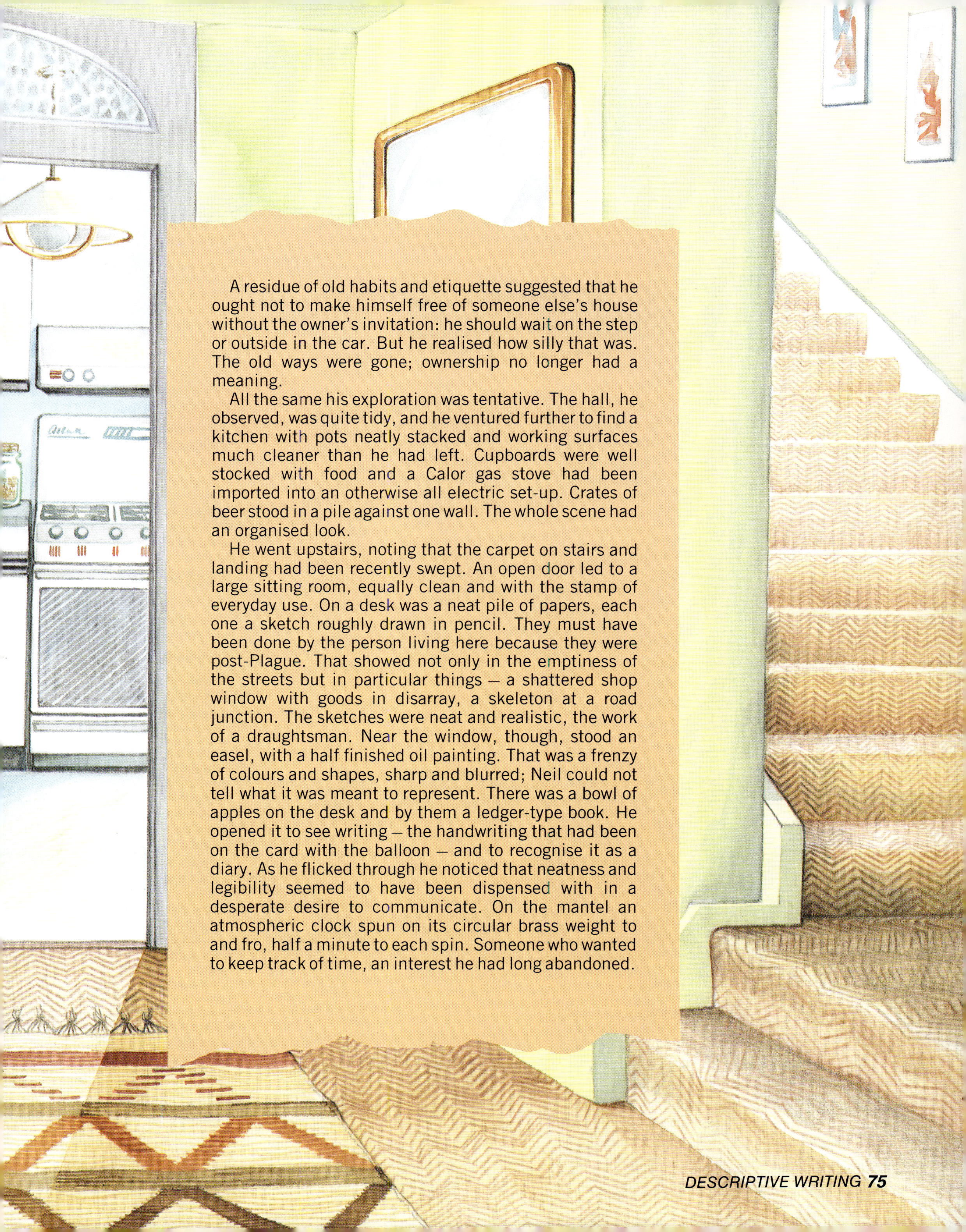

A residue of old habits and etiquette suggested that he ought not to make himself free of someone else's house without the owner's invitation: he should wait on the step or outside in the car. But he realised how silly that was. The old ways were gone; ownership no longer had a meaning.

All the same his exploration was tentative. The hall, he observed, was quite tidy, and he ventured further to find a kitchen with pots neatly stacked and working surfaces much cleaner than he had left. Cupboards were well stocked with food and a Calor gas stove had been imported into an otherwise all electric set-up. Crates of beer stood in a pile against one wall. The whole scene had an organised look.

He went upstairs, noting that the carpet on stairs and landing had been recently swept. An open door led to a large sitting room, equally clean and with the stamp of everyday use. On a desk was a neat pile of papers, each one a sketch roughly drawn in pencil. They must have been done by the person living here because they were post-Plague. That showed not only in the emptiness of the streets but in particular things – a shattered shop window with goods in disarray, a skeleton at a road junction. The sketches were neat and realistic, the work of a draughtsman. Near the window, though, stood an easel, with a half finished oil painting. That was a frenzy of colours and shapes, sharp and blurred; Neil could not tell what it was meant to represent. There was a bowl of apples on the desk and by them a ledger-type book. He opened it to see writing – the handwriting that had been on the card with the balloon – and to recognise it as a diary. As he flicked through he noticed that neatness and legibility seemed to have been dispensed with in a desperate desire to communicate. On the mantel an atmospheric clock spun on its circular brass weight to and fro, half a minute to each spin. Someone who wanted to keep track of time, an interest he had long abandoned.

He continued with his exploration. There was a bathroom across the way, again very clean, with a kettle in which hot water had presumably been carried up from the kitchen. The best solution, he decided, would be for both of them to abandon their present dens — to join in finding a place where a full hot water system, perhaps central heating as well, could be run off Calor gas. He was pleased with himself for the thought: he could be enterprising as well.

The door of the next room was ajar. Neil pushed it open and saw that the curtains were drawn and it was in shadow. He saw a bed made up, the whiteness of sheets . . . then the darker vertical shadow that hung in the centre of the room. The rope was secured to an old-fashioned brass light fitting; a chair was overturned on the carpet.

He just managed to reach the bathroom before being sick.

Neil pulled out his handkerchief and wiped his face and mouth. Bitter disappointment and an overwhelming feeling of nausea crushed him. He stumbled out of the house and back into the car. His head slumped against the wheel and he wept. Long shudders convulsed his body until he fell into a disturbed sleep.

When he awoke it was daybreak and the silence was all around. How he hated that absence of sound and noise. His self-pity turned to anger. 'Damn him!' Why did he do it? How could he be so thoughtless and stupid? Why couldn't he have held on for one more day?

Neil knew he would have to go back into the house. He needed Calor gas and the food and beer would save a risky trip into town and so conserve his precious petrol. Yet he felt considerable unease as he pushed open the door and looked round the neat house where only a single chair was out of place.

Here are two empathic responses to the extract from *Empty World*, written by 16 year-old students. The first is the start of a continuation to the story. The second consists of a number of entries from the dead man's diary – which is mentioned in the story. As you read them, see how the writers have used information and detail from the extract in their own writing.

**Monday 2 May**

Three weeks now since the plague first hit this country. I've seen no living person since my housekeeper died 4 days ago. Drove into town today and made some sketches. The scenes are horrific but I'm sure that someone has to make a careful record of this disaster for those who come later. I've plenty of supplies stocked up. The worst things remain the loneliness and the boredom.

**Thursday 5 May**

Woke up in the night in a panic dreaming I heard a child crying. I was sweating heavily and stayed awake until dawn. There was no sound. During the day, I began another oil painting. The pain of the nightmare steered my brush. I still find work to do around the house but it all seems so pointless.

**Saturday 7 May**

I've given up hope. The balloons were my last good idea and they failed. I was fooling myself really. Painted over one of my street scenes today. The way the faces stared out of it – I couldn't stand it. I found myself talking to myself this morning as I sorted the stores. That's the first sign of madness, isn't it? I don't know what to do.

**Sunday 8 May**

Can't write today. There's no point. I read back in the diary and scribbled a lot out. I was so stupid thinking someone might come. I've been sitting watching the clock all afternoon. It goes on but time has stopped now. I think I know what to do.

**5** **Choose either response and continue the story from this point, using some of the details you have been given and adding your own ideas. As you draft your writing, share it with others in the group and help one another to make each piece of writing more authentic.**

**6** **Use the extract as the starting point for a reflective poem with one of these titles:**

ALL ALONE
THE EMPTY WORLD
PLAGUE

## REWIND

- Almost all writing is descriptive in some way. Always look for ways to add appropriate description to your writing.
- Watch out for the shift of focus in deciding whether you are being asked to write description or reflection.
- Make sure that empathic writing is clearly related to the original information which inspired it.

6

# How it works and what to do!

## EXPLANATION AND INSTRUCTION

The three items illustrated on this page can be found in many houses. And if you were given a bicycle, a wine bottle and a videotape, you would probably have little difficulty in pumping up the tyres, opening the bottle and watching the video. But if you were asked to write down an explanation of how the bicycle pump works, that might prove to be much more of a challenge. Or if you were asked to explain how to program the video recorder, to someone who had never used one, that might be harder still. This section is about explanations, directions and instructions and how to put them down in writing.

### COLLECTING EVIDENCE . . .

You become a better writer by understanding what you are doing as you write. To look closely at these writing types, first provide yourself with some examples.

**1 Work with a partner. Each write one of the following. Talk about them first. Aim to write between 50 and 100 words.**

- ☐ how to make scrambled eggs
- ☐ how to travel by car from your school to the nearest railway station
- ☐ how to play noughts and crosses
- ☐ how to start off on a skateboard
- ☐ how a windmill grinds corn.

**2 Now answer one of these questions. Once again, discuss them with your partner but only spend a few minutes writing your answer. It does not have to be too detailed.**

- ☐ Why does a bicycle have gears?
- ☐ Why do some schools have uniforms for their pupils?
- ☐ Why do birds migrate?
- ☐ Why is the earth's climate thought to be changing?

## ANALYSING YOUR RESULTS

Between you, you should now have four samples of writing to look at more closely. If possible, exchange your samples with another pair's so that the writing you analyse was written by someone else.

**3** **Copy the chart below. Then answer the questions for each of your samples by ticking the columns headed A and B. If you cannot answer the question, leave the column blank.**

| **Questions** | **Samples of writing** | | | |
|---|---|---|---|---|
| | **One A : B** | **Two A : B** | **Three A : B** | **Four A : B** |
| **1** Do either of these words appear in the sample more than once? **a** I **b** you | | | | |
| **2** Do these words appear in the sample? **a** because or therefore **b** then or afterwards | | | | |
| **3** Are sections in the sample numbered or sub-headed? **a** no **b** yes | | | | |
| **4** Is the writing **a** non-chronological? **b** chronological? | | | | |
| **5** Is the writing **a** about a subject? **b** aimed at a reader? | | | | |
| **6** Is the writing **a** saying how something is done? **b** telling you why it is? | | | | |
| **7** Do the verbs mostly describe **a** actions? **b** thoughts and ideas? | | | | |
| **8** Does the writing give any commands or imperatives like 'Do this' or 'Go . . .'? **a** no **b** yes | | | | |
| **9** Is the reader addressed as if he or she is doing something? **a** no **b** yes | | | | |
| **10** Does the writing use scientific or technical terms? **a** yes – more than once **b** hardly ever – once or less | | | | |

Now check your results. For each sample, if the answers are mostly As, then the writing is probably explanation. If the answers are mostly Bs, then the writing is likely to be instructional. Compare your results with the original writer and your group. See how far you agree.

# EXPLANATION

You may be asked to write explanations in school for a wide range of subjects. You may be asked to:

- **Suggest the causes of . . .**
- **Explain how . . .**
- **Describe and explain . . .**
- **Explain the significance of . . .**
- **What were the causes of . . .**
- **Give reasons for . . .**
- **Use data to explain . . .**
- **Explain the features of . . .**

## WHY DO WE KISS?

**Kissing is merely a way for lovers to test each other's semiochemicals. These are chemical substances that communicate biological signals between animals and which are produced by the sebaceous glands in the skin. Falling in love may only be a 'high' caused by addiction to another person's semiochemicals.**

## WHY DOES GLUE STICK THINGS TOGETHER?

**Glue contains chemicals. When glue sets, the chemicals change and become new chemicals that pull very strongly on things. When you stick something with glue, it pulls the two parts together so strongly that they become fixed to the glue and therefore to each other.**

## WHY CAN YOU SEE YOURSELF IN A MIRROR?

**You can see yourself in a mirror because light rays bounce off its shiny surface. Light rays come from everything you can see, including yourself. You see things when the light rays from them enter your eyes. Some of the light rays that come from yourself strike the mirror. The mirror reflects the rays because it is very smooth. The rays come back to you and enter your eyes.**

## AFTER DRINKING A LOT OF ALCOHOL, WHY DOES THE ROOM SPIN?

**The spinning sensation is caused by alcohol in the blood upsetting the semicircular canals of the inner ear, which sense balance. This effect can also occur when these organs become infected. When in the northern hemisphere, the room will appear to swim clockwise; in the southern hemisphere, the room will spin anticlockwise!**

## CAN AIDS BE TRANSMITTED BY MOSQUITOES?

**If blood-sucking insects did inject the blood obtained from one person into another, they might transmit Aids. Fortunately, they don't. They inject a saliva secretion which contains an anticlotting agent to prevent blocking the tube through which the blood is obtained. There is no evidence that the Aids virus can get into the mosquito's salivary glands.**

**4** **Although expressed differently, these tasks have many features in common. This page shows different pieces of writing which 'explain' how things work or are caused. Pick two of them and write a commentary on each one describing the features they have which tell you they are examples of explanatory writing. Use the chart on the previous page to help you.**

**5** **These numbered illustrations show a range of common errors which first-time photographers often make. Imagine that they are to be used to illustrate a magazine article for young people with very little knowledge of photography. Write a suitable caption (about 50 words) for each one explaining what has gone wrong.**

1

2

3

4

5

## FACTFILE 8 EXPLANATION

When you are asked to give an explanation remember that:

- the writing should *focus* on reasons and causes
- the *purpose* of the writing is to answer the questions 'Why?' or 'How?'
- your *audience* can be anyone and the extent of their knowledge (what they know) should influence what you write
- you should use the present tense unless you are writing about events in the past
- you may need to use connectives which link a cause and effect like 'because', 'for this reason' or 'therefore'
- you should not use technical terms without explaining them.

**6** **The series of diagrams below shows how the moon appears from the Earth to change shape each night. Using the information it gives you, write your explanation of how this happens.**

# INSTRUCTIONS AND ADVICE

**7** **Collect together as many 'sets' of instructions as you can find. Try to find examples of the instructions that come with electrical goods, road directions, recipes, textbook assignments and photocopy them. Use the questions with the chart on page 79 to help you annotate them and show some of their features.**

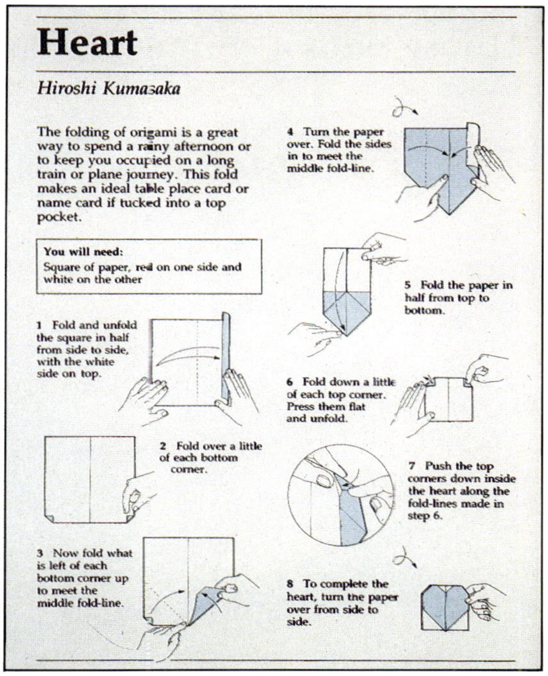

## Heart

*Hiroshi Kumasaka*

The folding of origami is a great way to spend a rainy afternoon or to keep you occupied on a long train or plane journey. This fold makes an ideal table place card or name card if tucked into a top pocket.

**You will need:**
Square of paper, red on one side and white on the other

1 Fold and unfold the square in half from side to side, with the white side on top.

2 Fold over a little of each bottom corner.

3 Now fold what is left of each bottom corner up to meet the middle fold-line.

4 Turn the paper over. Fold the sides in to meet the middle fold-line.

5 Fold the paper in half from top to bottom.

6 Fold down a little of each top corner. Press them flat and unfold.

7 Push the top corners down inside the heart along the fold-lines made in step 6.

8 To complete the heart, turn the paper over from side to side.

**The Scientific Committee on Antarctic Research (SCAR) which is part of the Antarctic Treaty System recommends the following guidelines:**

- Remember that the vegetation is fragile and very slow-growing. Avoid walking over moss-banks or lichen-covered scree slopes.
- Do not collect conspicuous lichens or moss tufts. The best souvenirs to bring back from the Antarctic are memories and photographs.
- Do not collect fossils, other interesting mineral specimens, or disturb patterned ground. Remember: these features are irreplaceable on a human time-scale.
- Do not disturb nesting bird colonies. Stay outside the margins of a colony and observe from a distance.
- Do not disturb sleeping seals and never attempt to handle seal pups. The bonds between mother and pup can easily be disrupted and the survival of the pup is jeopardised.
- Avoid marked sites where scientific experiments are going on. Remember that these experiments represent somebody's professional work – and have cost some government (perhaps yours) a great deal of money. Respect the scientists' interests and careers.
- Take all litter back to the ship with you. It takes decades for it to break down in the Antarctic environment.

## Better safe than sorry

If you go to an area where alligators or crocodiles are known, there are some precautions you should take.

1 Always pay attention to notices warning of the danger of crocodiles or alligators. You will probably never see an alligator or crocodile but they are there, hidden under the water.
2 If you go on holiday to a new place, always check with local people whether alligators or crocodiles have ever been seen.
3 Do not allow small children or dogs to paddle or wade in the water.
4 Do not think that a shallow pool or even a drainage canal nearby is safe. Alligators and crocodiles sometimes travel some distance from one body of water to another. They can lie hidden in water as shallow as 30cm (12 inches) for more than an hour.
5 Always stand at least 3m (10 feet) from the water's edge when fishing. Remember alligators and crocodiles are amphibious and can lunge onto land.
6 Do not gut fish into the water or dump bait into it. These scraps will attract alligators and crocodiles.
7 If you are in a boat, do not dangle your legs or arms in the water.
8 If you see a hatchling alligator or crocodile in the water, leave the area immediately. The adults will probably be close by.
9 Always use a torch when walking near the water's edge at night. The eyes of an alligator or crocodile glow red in a beam of light. But even if you do not see the red eyeshine, be careful! An alligator or crocodile could still be submerged and invisible under a jetty or tree at the water's edge.

## *FACTFILE 9* INSTRUCTIONS

If you are asked to write instructions or advice remember that:

- the *focus* of the writing is on the reader and their actions so that their knowledge or experience will shape what you write
- the *purpose* of the writing is to give information which another person can follow
- the *audience* can be any number of people – from a single person to an unknown group but you must know exactly who it is before you start to write
- the writing must be organised in a series of chronological steps or sequences
- you can use imperatives to 'tell' your reader what to do
- you will need to use verbs which describe action and movements
- you will need to link sentences with words like 'now' and 'then', or phrases like 'after this'.

# ROOT th

This is the board for a game for two players called 'Root the Loot' but the instructions on how to play the game are missing. The idea of the game is that one player controls three ferrets who try to stop three moles (controlled by the other player) from 'rooting the loot' – the scouts' supplies – in the tents on the surface. The object of the game is to stop the moles from stealing too much food on their raids.

The game is played twice and the person whose moles 'rooted' most food is the winner. The game uses six marked counters – for the moles and ferrets – and a die. You also need a pen and pencil to keep the score.

**8 With your partner try to work out the rules for how to play 'Root the Loot'. You will need to think about:**

- ☐ where the moles and ferrets start from
- ☐ what a 'move' is
- ☐ whether the moles and ferrets move at the same speed
- ☐ how to keep score.

When you have finished, write your version of the rules which could be published with this game. Swap them with another pair and then play the game *their* way. Note down where their instructions are confusing or leave out important information. At the end of the session compare notes before looking at the actual rules which are printed on page 128.

**9** **Here is a set of instructions showing how to operate a video camcorder. However the text is in Japanese. Working from the diagrams, write a set of instructions which would help a new purchaser to operate the camera.**

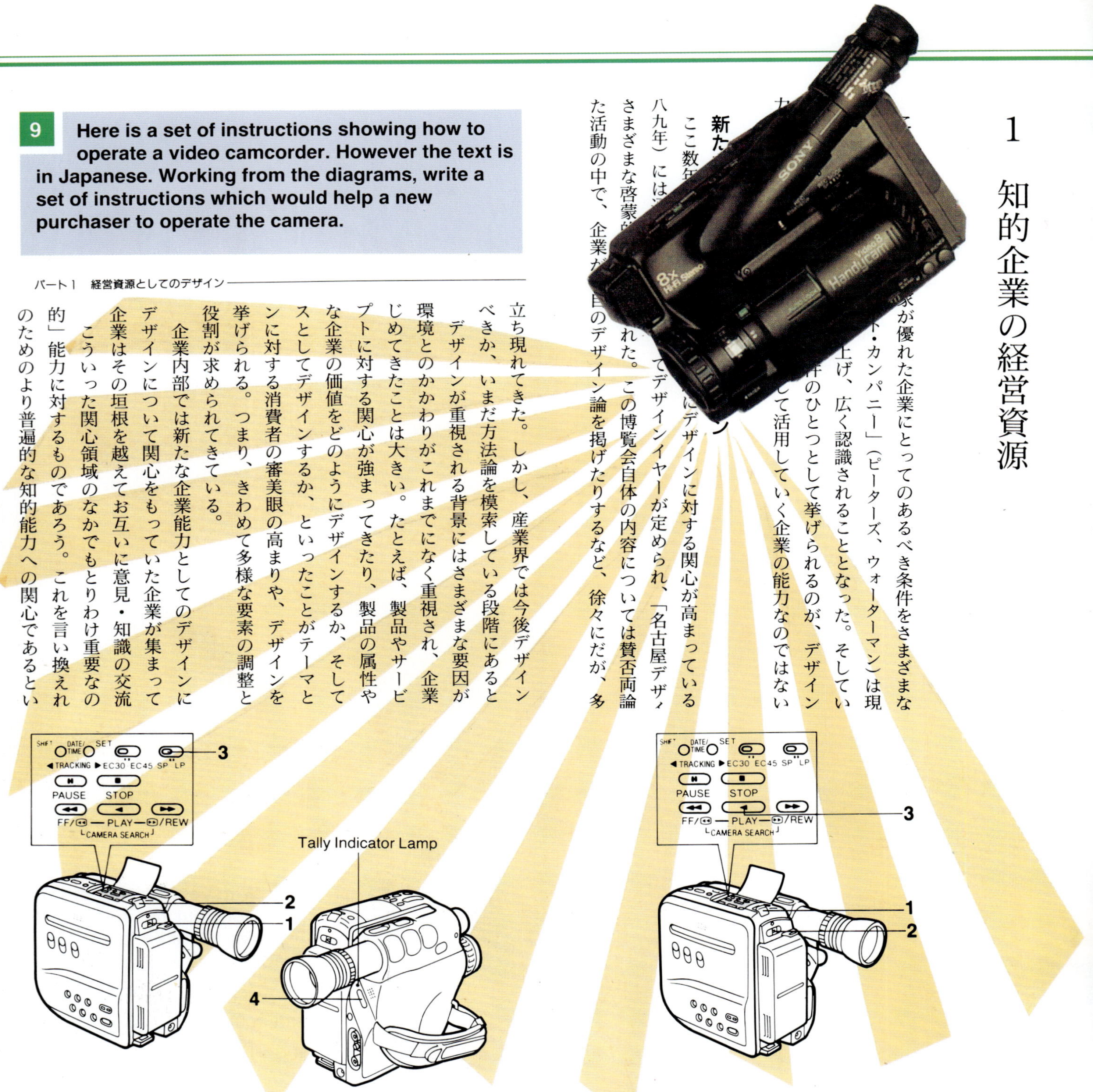


**10** **Finally, look back through your own recent work in all your school subjects and find an occasion when you were asked to present information in any of the ways you have thought about as you worked through this section. Using what you know about that type of writing, write about what you did well and what you might have done better or in more detail. Then, redraft and revise your writing and display the two pieces of work together.**

### REWIND

- When asked for an explanation, make sure that you have a clear understanding of the reasons and causes you are describing before you begin to write.
- As you write instructions, remember that leaving out a single step in the process may mean that your reader gets lost.

# 7

# Telling tales

## *WRITING NARRATIVE*

The most widely used writing type and the first that children from any culture encounter is the story, or narrative. Parents tell their children 'stories' and, almost as soon as they can write, young children are encouraged to write stories – sometimes imaginary and sometimes based on their own experiences. As you have gone through school, you will have told or written stories and narratives on many occasions and listened to them being told or read to you. This section explores how narratives, like any other writing type, can be analysed in terms of their focus, purpose and audience and the kinds of language features they reveal.

**1** **The four extracts on pages 88–95 are all very different but they are all, in their own ways, narratives. Read them through and talk about them in groups. For each piece of writing decide on:**

- ☐ the focus of the writing
- ☐ the writer's purpose
- ☐ the audience who it is written for.

**As you talk, try to identify any language features of the writing which help you to come to your conclusion. You might think about:**

- ☐ the ways that parts of the writing are organised or linked
- ☐ the length and complexity of the sentences
- ☐ the vocabulary used
- ☐ the description used in the writing.

They were strolling along the high road, the Mole by the horse's head; the Toad and the Water Rat walking behind the cart talking together – at least Toad was talking, and Rat was thinking all the time of something very different.

Then far behind them they heard a faint warning hum, like the drone of a distant bee. Glancing back, they saw a small cloud of dust, with a dark centre, advancing on them at incredible speed, while from out of the dust a faint 'Poop-poop!' wailed like an uneasy animal in pain. In an instant the peaceful scene was changed, and with a blast of wind and a whirl of sound that made them jump for the nearest ditch, it was on them! The 'poop-poop' rang with a blaring shout in their ears, they had a moment's glimpse of a magnificent motor-car – breath-snatching, passionate, with its driver tense as he hugged his wheel – it claimed all earth and air for a fraction of a second. It flung a cloud of dust that blinded and enwrapped them, utterly, and then dwindled to a speck in the far distance, changed back into a droning bee once more.

The old grey horse simply abandoned himself to

his natural emotions. Rearing, plunging, backing steadily, in spite of all the Mole's efforts at his head, and all the Mole's lively language appealing to his better nature, he drove the cart backwards towards the deep ditch at the side of the road. It wavered an instant – then there was a heartrending crash – and the cart, their pride and their joy, lay on its side in the ditch, a complete wreck.

The Rat danced up and down in the road, simply transported with passion. 'You villains!' he shouted, shaking both fists. 'You scoundrels, you highwaymen, you road-hogs! I'll have the law on you! I'll report you! I'll take you through all the Courts!'



Toad sat straight down in the middle of the dusty road, his legs stretched out before him, and stared fixedly in the direction of the disappearing motor-car. He breathed short, his face wore a placid, satisfied expression, and at intervals he faintly murmured, 'Poop-poop!'

The Mole was busy trying to quiet the horse, which he succeeded in doing after a time. Then he went to look at the cart, on its side in the ditch. It was indeed a sorry sight. Panels and windows smashed, axles hopelessly bent, one wheel off, and sardine-tins scattered over the wide world. The Rat came to help him, but their united efforts were not sufficient to right the cart. 'Hi! Toad!' they cried. 'Come and bear a hand, can't you?'

The Toad never answered a word, or budged from his seat in the road; so they went to see what was the matter with him. They found him in a sort of trance, a happy smile on his face, his eyes still fixed on the dusty wake of their destroyer. At intervals he was heard to murmur 'Poop-poop!'

The Rat shook him by the shoulder. 'Are you coming to help us, Toad?' he demanded sternly.

'Glorious, stirring sight!' murmured Toad,



never offering to move. 'The poetry of motion! The *real* way to travel! The *only* way to travel! Here today – in next week tomorrow! Villages skipped, towns and cities jumped! O bliss! O poop-poop! Oh my! Oh! my!'

'O stop being a fool, Toad!' cried the Mole.

(from *The Wind in the Willows* by Kenneth Grahame)

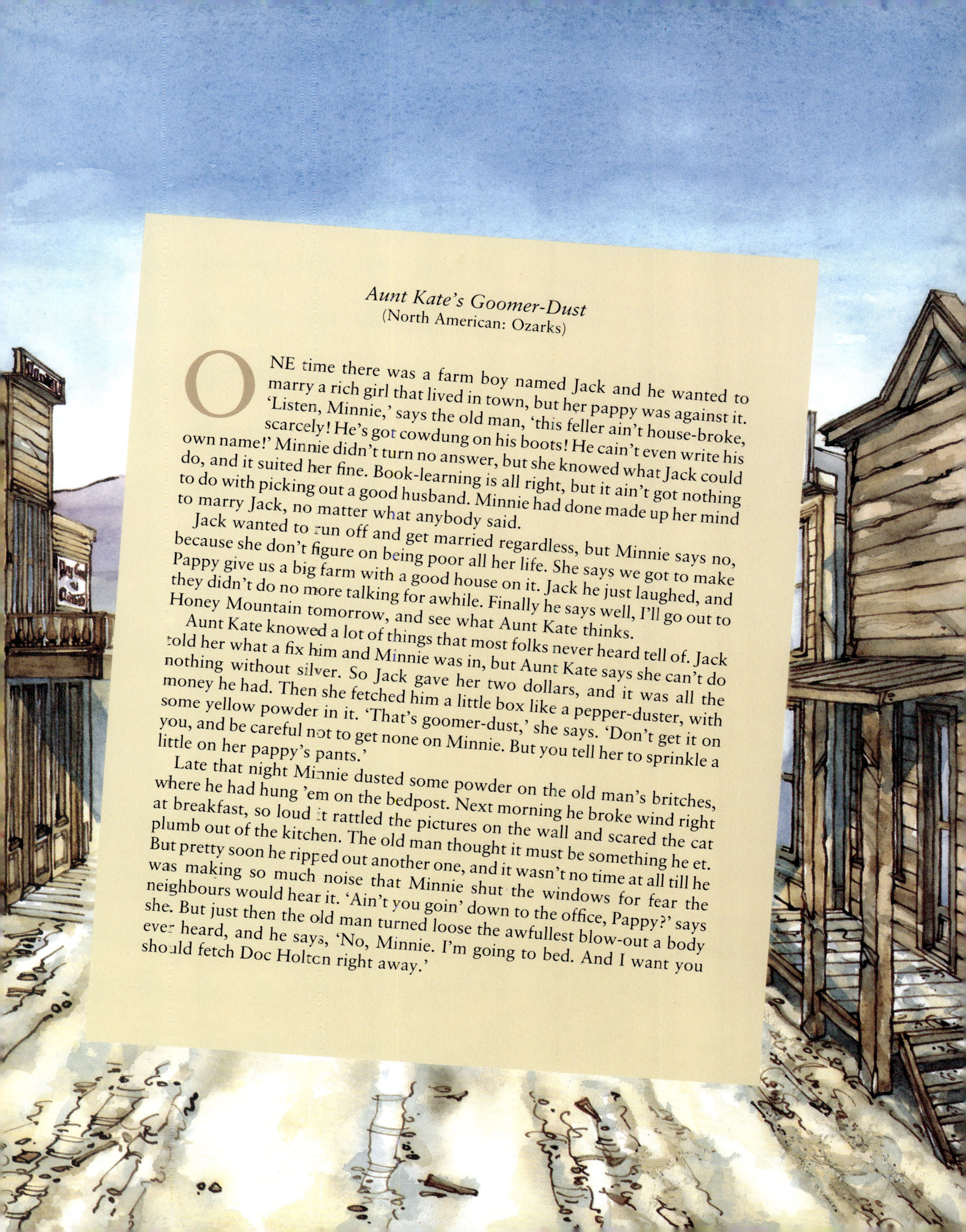

*Aunt Kate's Goomer-Dust*
(North American: Ozarks)

ONE time there was a farm boy named Jack and he wanted to marry a rich girl that lived in town, but her pappy was against it. 'Listen, Minnie,' says the old man, 'this feller ain't house-broke, scarcely! He's got cowdung on his boots! He cain't even write his own name!' Minnie didn't turn no answer, but she knowed what Jack could do, and it suited her fine. Book-learning is all right, but it ain't got nothing to do with picking out a good husband. Minnie had done made up her mind to marry Jack, no matter what anybody said.

Jack wanted to run off and get married regardless, but Minnie says no, because she don't figure on being poor all her life. She says we got to make Pappy give us a big farm with a good house on it. Jack he just laughed, and they didn't do no more talking for awhile. Finally he says well, I'll go out to Honey Mountain tomorrow, and see what Aunt Kate thinks.

Aunt Kate knowed a lot of things that most folks never heard tell of. Jack told her what a fix him and Minnie was in, but Aunt Kate says she can't do nothing without silver. So Jack gave her two dollars, and it was all the money he had. Then she fetched him a little box like a pepper-duster, with some yellow powder in it. 'That's goomer-dust,' she says. 'Don't get it on you, and be careful not to get none on Minnie. But you tell her to sprinkle a little on her pappy's pants.'

Late that night Minnie dusted some powder on the old man's britches, where he had hung 'em on the bedpost. Next morning he broke wind right at breakfast, so loud it rattled the pictures on the wall and scared the cat plumb out of the kitchen. The old man thought it must be something he et. But pretty soon he ripped out another one, and it wasn't no time at all till he was making so much noise that Minnie shut the windows for fear the neighbours would hear it. 'Ain't you goin' down to the office, Pappy?' says she. But just then the old man turned loose the awfullest blow-out a body ever heard, and he says, 'No, Minnie. I'm going to bed. And I want you should fetch Doc Holton right away.'

When Doc got there Pappy was feeling better, but pretty white and shaky. 'Soon as I got in bed the wind died down,' he says, 'but it was terrible while it lasted,' and he told Doc all about what happened. Doc examined Pappy a long time and give him some medicine to make him sleep. Minnie follered Doc out on the porch, and Doc says, 'Did you hear them loud noises he keeps talkin' about, like somebody breakin' wind?' Minnie says no, she didn't hear nothing like that. 'Just as I thought,' says Doc. 'He just imagined the whole thing. There ain't nothing wrong with your pappy, only his nerves.'

Pappy slept pretty good, on account of the medicine Doc give him. But next morning, soon as he got up and put his clothes on, he begun to break wind worse than ever. Finally he fired off a blast that sounded like a ten-bore shotgun, so Minnie helped him back in bed and sent for the doctor. Doc give him a shot in the arm this time. 'Keep that man in bed,' says he, 'till I get Doctor Culberson to come over and look at him.' Both of them doctors examined Pappy from head to foot, but they couldn't find nothing wrong with him. They just shuck their heads, and give him some sleeping medicine.

Things went along like that for three days a-running, and finally Doc says Pappy better stay in bed all the time for awhile, and take medicine every four hours, and maybe he would be happier in a institution. 'Put me in the asylum, just because I got wind on the guts?' yelled Pappy. And with that he begun to raise such a row the doctor had to give him another shot in the arm.

Next morning Pappy set up in bed a-hollering how the doctors are all damn fools, and Minnie says she knows a fellow that can cure him in five minutes. Pretty soon Jack come a-walking in. 'Yes, I can cure you easy,' he says, 'but you got to let me and Minnie get married, and give us one of them big farms.' Pappy wouldn't even speak to Jack. 'If this halfwit cures me,' he says to Minnie, 'you can have any goddam thing you want.' Minnie walked over and stirred up the coals in the fireplace. Soon as it got to burning good, Jack took the tongs and throwed Pappy's britches right in the fire.

When Pappy seen them pants a-burning he was plumb speechless. He just laid there weak as a cat, and Jack marched out like a regular doctor. But after while the old man got up and put on his Sunday clothes. He never broke wind, neither. Minnie fixed him a fine breakfast, and he et every bite of it and never even belched. Then he walked round the house three times, without feeling no gas on his innards. 'Well, by God,' he says, 'I believe to my soul that damn fool did cure me!' On the way down town he stopped in to see Doc Holton. 'I finally got well, without no thanks to you,' says he. 'If you had your way, I'd be in the crazy-house this minute!'

Soon as he got Doc told, Pappy went over to the bank and deeded his best farm to Minnie. He give her some money to buy horses and cows and machinery. And so her and Jack got married, and they done all right. Some folks say they lived happy ever after.

## CHAPTER X

*one*

SHE'D been terrified the summer before, when it was discovered that white soldiers had come into the country. The band had never met the hair mouths, except for killing several on isolated occasions. She had hoped they would never meet them.

When the white soldiers' horses were stolen late last summer, she had panicked and run off. She was sure the white soldiers would come to the village. But they didn't.

Still, she was on pins and needles until it was determined that, without their horses, the white soldiers were practically helpless. Then she had been able to relax a little. But it wasn't until they broke camp and were on the winter trail that the awful cloud of fear that followed her all summer finally lifted.

Now summer was on them again, and all along the trail from the winter camp she had prayed fiercely for the hair mouths to be gone. Her prayers had not been answered, and once again her days were troubled, hour by hour.

Her name was Stands With A Fist.

She alone, among all the Comanches, knew that the white man was not a god. The story of Kicking Bird's encounter did puzzle her, however. A single naked white man? Out here? In the Comanche homeland? It didn't make sense. But no matter. Without knowing precisely why, she knew he was not a god. Something old told her so.

She heard the story that morning, on her way to the once-a-month lodge, the one set aside for menstruating women. She'd been thinking of her husband. Normally she did not like going to the lodge because she would miss his company. He was wonderful, a brave, handsome, and altogether exceptional man. A model husband. She had never been struck by him, and though both their babies had died (one in childbirth, the other a few weeks later), he had stubbornly refused to take another wife.

People had urged him to take another wife. Even Stands With A Fist had suggested it. But he said simply, 'You are plenty,' and she had never spoken of it again. In her secret heart she was proud that he was happy with her alone.

She missed him terribly now. Before they broke winter camp he'd taken a large party against the Utes. Nearly a month had passed with no word of him or the other warriors. But because she was already cut off from him, going to the once-a-month lodge had not seemed as hard as usual. As she made ready to leave that morning, the young Comanche woman was comforted by the notion that a close friend or two would be sequestered with her, women with whom the time would pass easily.

But on her way to the lodge she heard of Kicking Bird's odd story. Then she heard the story of the foolish raid. Stands With A Fist's morning had exploded in her face. Once more a great dread had settled on her square, straight shoulders like an iron blanket, and she entered the once-a-month lodge badly shaken.

But she was very strong. Her beautiful light brown eyes, eyes that shone with intelligence, revealed nothing as she sewed and chatted through the morning with her friends.

They knew the danger. The whole band knew. But it served no one to talk about it. So no one did.

All afternoon her tough, tiny frame moved about the lodge, showing nothing of the heavy blanket hanging over it.

Stands With A Fist was twenty-six years old.

For almost twelve of those years she had been a Comanche.

Before that she had been . . . what was it?

She only thought of the name on the rare occasions when she could not avoid thinking about the whites. Then, for some inexplicable reason, it would pop up in front of her eyes.

Oh, yes, she thought in Comanche, I remember it. Before, I was Christine.

Then she would think of before, and it was always the same. It was like passing through an old, misty curtain and the two worlds became one, the old mingling with the new. Stands With A Fist was Christine and Christine was Stands With A Fist.

Her complexion had darkened over the years, and the whole of her appearance had a distinctly wild cast about it. But despite two full-term pregnancies, her figure was like that of a white woman. And her hair, which refused to grow beyond her shoulders and refused to stay straight, still held a pronounced cherry tint. And, of course, there were the two light brown eyes.

Stands With A Fist's great fear was well founded. She could never hope to escape it. To a white eye there would always be something strange about the woman in the once-a-month lodge. Something not altogether Indian. And to the knowing eyes of her own people there was something not altogether Indian, even after all this time.

It was a terrible, heavy burden, but Stands With A Fist never spoke of it, much less complained. She carried it silently and with great bravery through every day of her Indian life, and she carried it for one monumental reason.

Stands With A Fist wanted to stay where she was.

She was very happy.

(from *Dances with Wolves* by Michael Blake)

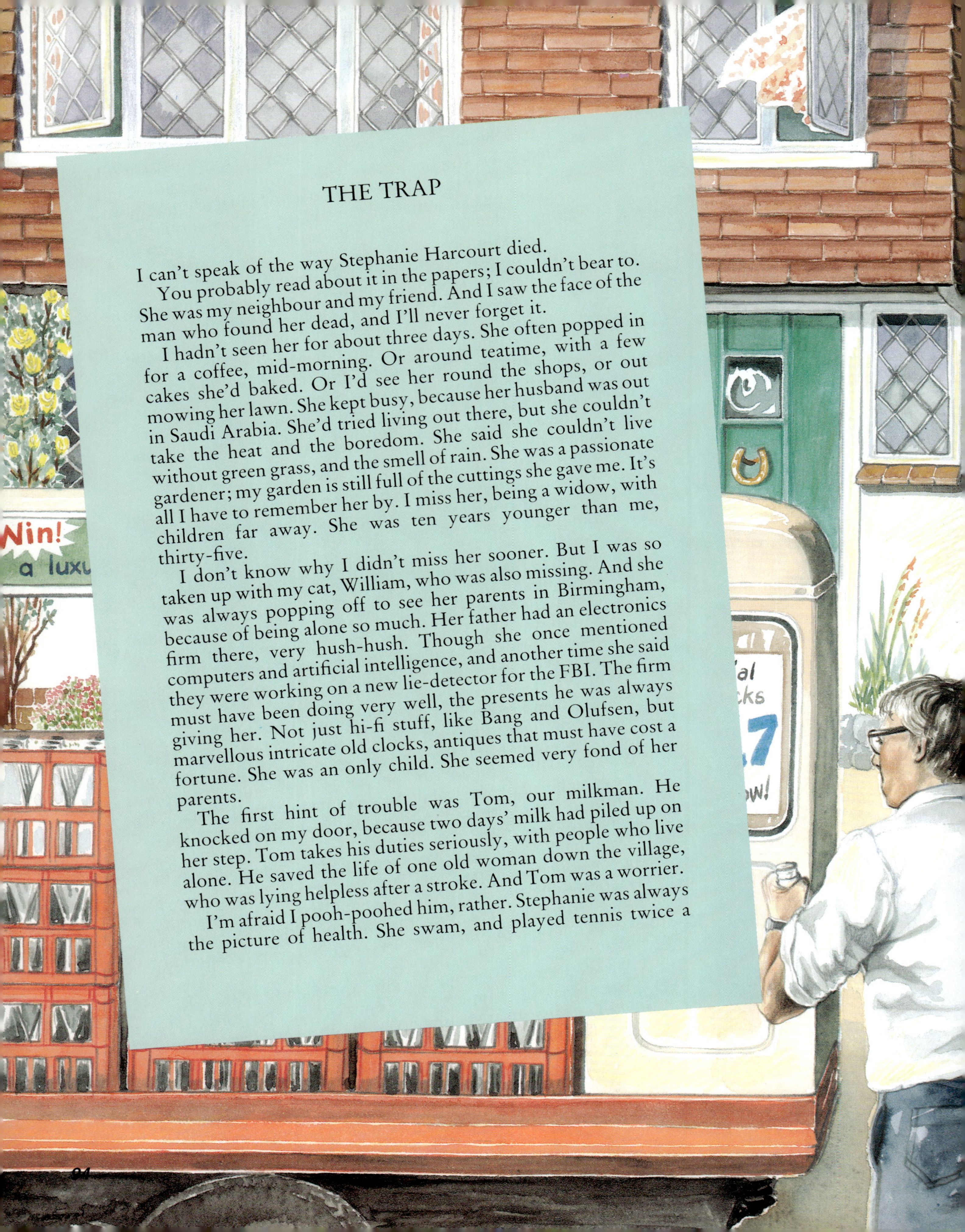

# THE TRAP

I can't speak of the way Stephanie Harcourt died.

You probably read about it in the papers; I couldn't bear to. She was my neighbour and my friend. And I saw the face of the man who found her dead, and I'll never forget it.

I hadn't seen her for about three days. She often popped in for a coffee, mid-morning. Or around teatime, with a few cakes she'd baked. Or I'd see her round the shops, or out mowing her lawn. She kept busy, because her husband was out in Saudi Arabia. She'd tried living out there, but she couldn't take the heat and the boredom. She said she couldn't live without green grass, and the smell of rain. She was a passionate gardener; my garden is still full of the cuttings she gave me. It's all I have to remember her by. I miss her, being a widow, with children far away. She was ten years younger than me, thirty-five.

I don't know why I didn't miss her sooner. But I was so taken up with my cat, William, who was also missing. And she was always popping off to see her parents in Birmingham, because of being alone so much. Her father had an electronics firm there, very hush-hush. Though she once mentioned computers and artificial intelligence, and another time she said they were working on a new lie-detector for the FBI. The firm must have been doing very well, the presents he was always giving her. Not just hi-fi stuff, like Bang and Olufsen, but marvellous intricate old clocks, antiques that must have cost a fortune. She was an only child. She seemed very fond of her parents.

The first hint of trouble was Tom, our milkman. He knocked on my door, because two days' milk had piled up on her step. Tom takes his duties seriously, with people who live alone. He saved the life of one old woman down the village, who was lying helpless after a stroke. And Tom was a worrier.

I'm afraid I pooh-poohed him, rather. Stephanie was always the picture of health. She swam, and played tennis twice a

week. And we weren't a worrying sort of district; a large village full of big old houses, and no council estates full of the unemployed within ten miles. People were still a bit sloppy about locking their doors, then. We didn't even have a Neighbourhood Watch Scheme.

I told Tom not to worry; she must have forgotten to cancel the milk. I even asked him to keep an eye open for William. Then I went and collected the milk off Stephanie's doorstep. It was a beautiful morning in June, and her lawn was just beginning to re-sprout daisies. Somehow, that convinced me she must be away; she was very regular with the lawn-mower. I remember how nice the sun looked on her front door. There was no hint of what lay behind it. The first day's milk had gone off, pushing the cap up with a column of clogged sour cream. But the second day's was usable. I hate waste.

As I was picking up the bottles, my cat William came strolling home, looking as pleased as Punch with himself.

That was the last good news I had for a long time.

The next thing was a ring on my front doorbell. Ring, ring, ring. I stamped down the front hall calling, 'All right, all right. Where's the fire?'

I opened the door, and a very young policeman was standing there. Swaying. Holding himself up with one hand on my ornamental urn. His face was so white that his freckles stood out like bloodspots. He was staring at something over my left shoulder. He moved his lips and nothing came out. I helped him into my lounge, thinking he'd been taken ill. He fell into my sofa, then suddenly bent over and was sick all over my Persian rug.

I still couldn't get any sense out of him. He just went on staring and shivering. So I reached for my cordless phone, and dialled 999 and reported a policeman in distress. Even then, I was ironically amused. The rug was probably ruined, but insured. I was already shaping the whole thing into an amusing story for the tennis-club . . .

(from a story by Robert Westall)

# ANALYSING NARRATIVE

No two narratives are quite the same and the study of narrative writing as a genre is extremely complex. Even the experts disagree about exactly what is a narrative and what is not. However, it is possible to pick out some common features in the way people tell and write stories which can help you to become a better writer.

**I am born**

In consideration of the day and hour of my birth, it was declared by the nurse, and by some sage women in the neighbourbood who had taken a lively interest in me several months before there was any possibility of our becoming personally acquainted, first, that I was destined to be unlucky in life; and secondly, that I was privileged to see ghosts and spirits; both these gifts inevitably attaching, as they believed, to all unlucky infants of either gender, born towards the small hours on a Friday night.

(from *David Copperfield* by Charles Dickens)

**1801**

I have just returned from a visit to my landlord – the solitary neighbour that I shall be troubled with. This is certainly a beautiful country! In all England, I do not believe that I could have fixed on a situation so completely removed from the stir of society. A perfect misanthropist's heaven: and Mr Heathcliff and I are such a suitable pair to divide the desolation between us. A capital fellow! He little imagined how my heart warmed towards him when I beheld his black eyes withdraw so suspiciously under their brows, as I rode up, and when his fingers sheltered themselves, with a jealous resolution, still further in his waistcoat, as I announced my name.

'Mr Heathcliff!' I said.

A nod was the answer.

(from *Wuthering Heights* by Emily Brontë)

It was a graveyard of the old-fashioned western kind. It was on a hill, about a mile and a half from the village. It had a crazy board fence round it, which leaned inward in places, and outward the rest of the time, but stood upright nowhere. Grass and weeds grew rank over the whole cemetery. All the old graves were sunken in. There was not a tombstone on the place; round-topped, worm-eaten boards staggered over the graves, leaning for support and finding none. 'Sacred to the memory of' so-and-so had been painted on them once, but it could no longer have been read, on the most of them, now, even if there had been light.

A faint wind moaned through the trees, and Tom feared it might be the spirits of the dead complaining at being disturbed. The boys talked little, and only under their breath, for the time and the place and the pervading solemnity and silence oppressed their spirits. They found the sharp new heap they were seeking, and ensconced themselves within the protection of three great elms that grew in a bunch within a few feet of the grave.

Then they waited in silence for what seemed a long time. The hooting of a distant owl was all the sound that troubled the dead stillness.

(from *Tom Sawyer* by Mark Twain)

*Who tells the story?* In any narrative, there has to be a narrator – the person who tells the story. Usually, the narrator and the writer are the same person but the writer can make a character, or even a number of characters, in a book tell the story.

*How is the story told?* A narrator usually relates events as they might have happened in reality – as if he or she is looking back on what took place. But, sometimes, the events in a story are described as if they are taking place in the present. The narrator may also be part of the events or outside what is happening and may know more, less or about as much as the characters around him or her. The position of the narrator in relation to a story is known as the *stance* of the narrative.

*How is the story organised?* The structure of narratives can be very simple and comes from the way people speak when they tell one another about things which have happened. First, they set the scene and talk about the setting and the characters. Then, some events or action unfolds. Finally, these events are completed or resolved by an ending.

*What is the focus for the story?* Surprisingly, the focus of a narrative is not on the events or plot but on the reader. The reader's responses are what the writer focuses on and events are used to create a particular set of feelings in the reader's mind.

*What is the purpose in writing stories?* Different writing types can usually be told apart by their purpose but that is not the case with narratives. Their main purpose is to hold the reader's attention but they do this in a variety of ways, including entertaining, shocking, arousing or scaring.

*Who are the audiences for stories?* The audience can be extremely general – possibly just 'people who like this kind of story' – but may sometimes be very specific as, for example, in the child's storybook on page 88.

*What language features do stories have?* Some of the language features you might expect to find in a narrative include extensive description of the setting, the development of characters, the use of direct speech and a number of events described in a chronological way. You might also expect to find a clear ending, or resolution, and an exciting climax.

**2** **In a small group, discuss some of the narratives you have read recently in school or at home. Who tells the story in each of them? Can you identify a particular narrative stance? Can you say anything about their purpose or audience?**

**If you have read any of these well-known children's stories, can you say anything about the way they use these narrative features?**

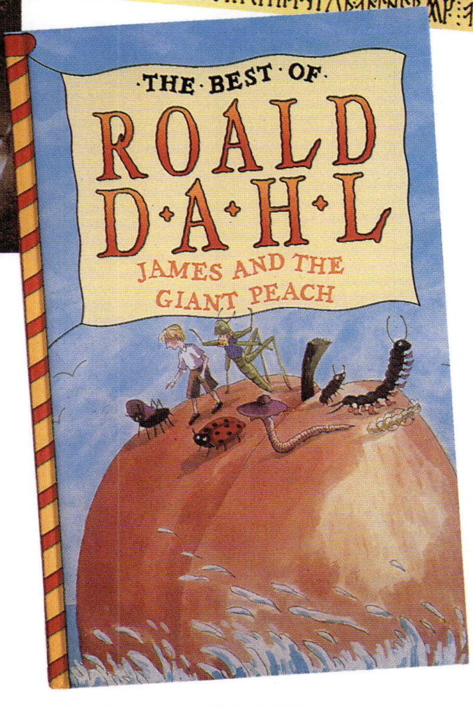

# LEVELS OF NARRATIVE

Below are some ideas for a murder story taken from a well-known writer's notebook. To help his writing, Ted Allsop and his girlfriend, Ellen McKay, stayed in an isolated house in Cumbria looking after it while the owner, Lady Darnley, was abroad. In a group of four or five, talk about the writer's thoughts and ideas about his writing and the kind of narrative they might lead to.

OCTOBER 14

It's great here ... quiet and isolated – a fantastic place for me to work without distraction. I'm ready to start writing now. Maybe Ellen and I will get on better than when we were in London.

OCTOBER 31

Snowed again today. We're really cut off as Little Darnley village is over 2 miles away. Ellen has been browsing in the library finding out about the family who lived here. Funny lot – the Darnleys. Old Lady Darnley had a huge family at one time but now they've all gone. No wonder she was so funny with me at the interview: wanted to know whether we had children and asked to see a photograph of Ellen. It was disconcerting having to say we couldn't have children – it isn't something you talk about. The latest Inspector Grant story isn't going well; I don't seem to have written 10 words in 3 weeks.

NOVEMBER 6

Something strange happened today. I thought Ellen was in the library so I went along to the scullery to make a cup of tea. As I was filling the kettle, I had this feeling there was someone else in the room. I turned round thinking it was Ellen but there was nobody there. You know how you think you see a flash of movement when that happens – some kind of optical illusion – I thought I saw a woman's outline. I called to Ellen half thinking it was her, but it wasn't.

NOVEMBER 12

Ellen says she heard someone screaming in the night – probably a fox got a rabbit. She was jumpy yesterday and it put me on edge. We almost bumped into each other walking round a corner and she got angry as if it was my fault and I was trying to scare her. I had that feeling again today – that sense of someone in the room. Maybe I am to blame. When you can't get the writing to flow it makes you angry inside.

NOVEMBER 14

Maybe I should dump Inspector Grant. There could be a story in this house. Ellen found an old newspaper – a copy of the 'Cumbrian Times' from 1951 and the lead article is about the trial of Edward Darnley, accused of the murder of his wife Eleanor. It's in front of me now. From what I can make out, he came back one night in December and found his wife with another man. There was an argument and she ended up stabbed to death.

NOVEMBER 15

That story must have got me in a mood yesterday. I was talking about it to Ellen after she'd been to the village and we got on to the question of Shaun. I pretend he's all right but deep down I hate him for what he did to Ellen and because of what happened to us. I said something about how I'd like to murder him and she was making

some sort of joke about it, something about how he'd be too strong for me. I felt she was laughing at me. Anyway, I started mapping out the Darnley story – something with the word 'faith' in the title. Maybe I could call the woman Faith as well, to connect them.

NOVEMBER 23

Well into writing now which is why I haven't written this journal for a few days. Faith Fearnley is a wild, extravagant woman who shortly after their marriage begins to spend her husband's fortune, and gets involved with gangland criminal Sean Kray. There's space for a chapter where she visits his East London haunts and is seen by one of the family servants who Sean has killed later. She and her husband Edward live in this remote stately home in Cornwall but he can't make her content with her lot. I was working late when Ellen came in and disturbed me. She called me Teddy (which I don't like) and asked was I coming to bed yet. I stayed up an extra hour just to show my work was more important and to spite her for putting me off!

DECEMBER 2

Tired today but forced myself to work while Ellen went to the village. She's been going down there a lot lately – more than she needs to just to get supplies. She says it's too quiet here – she gets bored while I'm working all hours. Never satisfied some people! Faith (i.e. Eleanor Darnley) has met Kray and brought him back to the house while Edward is out shooting. Quite a passionate scene follows. I think I managed to get the feeling across that Eleanor, for all her wealth, is a flash tart underneath. Edward is on his way back now – early because the fog is coming down. There's an odd presence in my study these days – as if someone is watching me work: sometimes there's a rustling sound – probably mice! There's also a sweet perfumey smell at times.

DECEMBER 5

Finished the first draft of 'Faith No More' this morning. Ellen had gone to town again! Fell asleep over the computer and had the weirdest dream. In the dream I was awake and this woman was by the study door beckoning me. I followed her down the corridor but somehow couldn't catch up with her. She stopped by the scullery door which was part open and there was Ellen embracing and kissing with some man. I awoke with a start. Felt decidedly nervy afterwards and when I made a sandwich later I took a carving knife back to the study with me. It was quite reassuring having it there by the word processor. Tomorrow I'll start the final draft.....

**3** **Talk with your group about what you have found out about 'Faith No More' and the kind of story it is. What might its effect be on a reader? What kind of readers would it appeal to? Then, turn over to read a section from the finished story.**

# Surprise! Surprise!

The last question was unfair. There never was a book called 'Faith No More' and Ted Allsop is not a famous writer. After being a writer for most of this book, you are now a reader and quite possibly you have been fooled.

**4** **Look at the writer's notebook again and discuss these questions as a group:**

- ☐ What made you think that the journal was genuine? The context it was placed in by this book? The opening statement about Ted Allsop? The way it read?
- ☐ What made you first think it was invented? The unlikelihood of the events? The parallels between them?
- ☐ Can you now see a story within the journal? Could there be more than one there? Could there be three?
- ☐ Can this journal be called a narrative? What features would say it could or could not be? For example, has it got an ending or does it just stop?

**Share your ideas with the rest of the group.**

**5** **Use the journal as the starting point for some narrative writing of your own. Write Ellen McKay's account of what happened, ending with her husband's madness and his attempt to kill her. You will have to use information from the journal as well as adding facts and description of your own. In doing this, you will be changing both the narrator and the stance of the narrative and developing a new purpose – perhaps to both frighten and entertain your reader.**

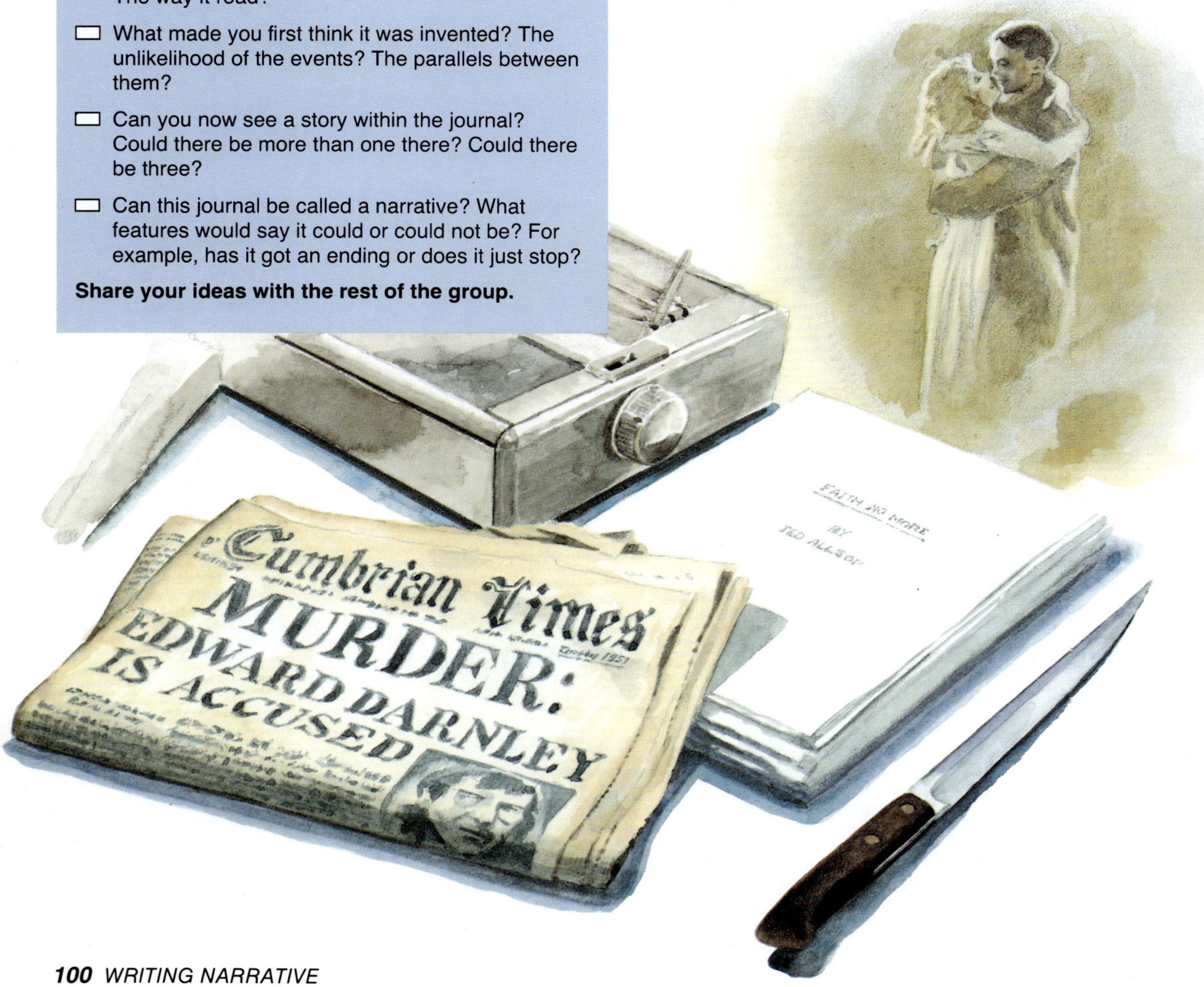

# I WAS THERE

As you have learned to analyse types of writing you have seen how the focus of the writing, its purpose and audience are the features that make writing types different. However, some types of writing mix the focus and the purpose of the writing in interesting ways. Autobiographical writing is one kind of narrative writing which does this and is also a type of writing that you will frequently be asked to read or write in school.

Starting from an eye-witness account, an autobiography gives the writer's personal view of events adding opinion and comment and making both the writer and the events into the focus of the writing.

I remember going to a place called Highcliffe where my granny had a bungalow made out of a railway carriage. It had a wood and glass front with windows all along it. Granny had her favourite chair at one end and used to sit there with her special brand of cigarettes – ones with the cat on the red packet – by her side. My bedroom was like a compartment with a big heavy door and 'No Smoking' engraved on the window. It smelt of salt and tar and the floors were always sandy.

**6** **In a small group, think back to some of the good times and places you remember. Tell one another about them, describing what you can recall of the place and the time.**

Everyday I took a short cut through the cemetery on my way to school. I often looked at the graves and thought about the people in them. Sometimes, I'd pretend I knew the person and tidy up all the weeds around their grave. I used to collect caterpillars there as well, or catch greenbottle flies and feed them to garden spiders. My sister took some green marble chips off a new grave once but then she got scared and put them back. There was one grave where a woman got buried alive and people heard her screams and dug her up again. I always ran past there.

**7** **Now write your own account of one of the incidents you remember from your discussion. In this autobiographical writing, the focus of the writing is on you, the writer, and your reactions to what happened. The setting will therefore have to be described in particular detail to help a reader understand what you felt. Use a first person ('I' or 'We') narrator but you may introduce other characters and direct speech.**

## FACTFILE 10 NARRATIVE

When you are asked to write stories or narratives remember that:

- the *focus* of the writing is on the reader and their response. A good story is one which a reader will feel involved in or be moved by in some way.
- the *purpose* of the writing can be to inform, to entertain, to amuse or just to grip the attention of a reader. It is important, however, that the writer knows exactly what he or she is trying to achieve.
- the *audience* can be very general – anyone who likes detective thrillers – or very specific, as in storybooks for very young readers.
- the *organisation* of narratives can be very varied but there is usually a chronological structure, a series of events or incidents involving some characters (the *plot*) and an ending where these are resolved (the *climax*).
- the main *language features* are description, particularly of characters (*characterisation*) and events, and the use of conversation between characters as part of the narrative (*direct speech*).

## ANALYSING YOUR WRITING

As you become a more practised writer, one of the things you begin to do is to understand the task requirements of a piece of writing. You do this by recognising what writing type is most appropriate to your task and by knowing what sort of features it possesses. So, if you were asked to write a section from your autobiography you would know immediately some of the features that writing might have. In the same way, if you were given an extract from a book to read, you might refer to those features to describe it as autobiographical.

**8** **With a partner, study these questions about writing features. Decide what you think the answers would be for an autobiography. Share your ideas with your group and see how far you agree.**

1 Will the writing be written in:
- A the third person
- B the second person
- C the first person?

2 Will the writing focus on:
- A events only
- B the writer only
- C the writer's part in events?

3 Will the writing be organised:
- A as an argument
- B in grouped sections according to its theme
- C in chronological sequence?

4 Will the writing be:
- A factual
- B descriptive
- C a mixture of the two?

5 Will the audience for the writing be:
- A the writer only
- B experts
- C anyone interested?

6 Is the main purpose of the writing:
- A to explain
- B to describe
- C to entertain?

Answering questions like these should help you see how sophisticated a writer you already are. Most of your answers should be Cs.

**9** **Read the following extract which is taken from the opening section of Bill Wyman's autobiography, *Stone Alone*. Write a commentary on the extract identifying where any of the features noted in task 8 occur in it.**

# Roots and Routes

But it is the sounds of wartime that live on in my mind. During the frequent air-raids, trucks with pom-pom guns went up and down the roads, firing shells at German planes. There were floating barrage balloons in every park and wasteland area. One day our milkman, making his deliveries during an air-raid, walked into an explosion and was blown up a flight of stairs, only to walk down again, completely unharmed. I remember one night raid when we had no time to get to the shelter. Mum threw herself over us children, all sleeping in one bed, as she heard the bombs fall. I suddenly realised that she really cared for us.

In early June 1944, when Rome had been captured and the Allies had landed in Normandy, Germany began its flying-bomb (V1 rocket) attacks on London. A neighbour, Mr Wheeler, took me out into the garden and showed me a flying bomb going over, with flames pouring from its back. Within a few weeks, we had our worst experience. We had gone to the shelter one day as the sirens sounded yet again. Mum had made sandwiches and drinks and we settled down in the damp, musty shelter to await the arrival of the flying bombs. We sat silently listening to the menacing drone, praying that they would pass overhead. The noise suddenly stopped right above us. The few seconds of silence seemed to last forever. Then a tremendous explosion made the ground shake. Dust and dirt, leaves and tree branches, were blown into the shelter. When the all-clear sounded we reappeared to a very different back-garden, with bushes and trees smashed, debris everywhere. Looking back at our house, we saw our huge French windows lying in the garden. The flying bomb had glided down two streets away, flattening about twenty houses. Inside every piece of furniture we had had been flung to the walls nearest the explosion.

My father was given five days' enemy-action leave and came home to arrange for mother and John, Anne and Judy, to be evacuated temporarily to Mansfield Woodhouse. I returned to my grandparents in Blenheim Road, Penge.

Shortly after this, when a flying bomb fell on Laurel Grove, just around the corner, I went to look with other kids, and found both sides of the street flattened. We rummaged through the rubble, picking up toys and books until we were chased off by air-raid personnel. It was only the next day at school that the harsh truth hit us: two girls in our class had been killed by that bomb.

It was a period when history was being made and a generation of kids had vital events etched on our subconscious minds, never to be completely forgotten. I remember a particularly exciting day earlier that year when all the local schools turned out and the children lined Maple Road. Winston Churchill visited us in a convoy of cars; he stood waving, making his victory sign and smoking his big cigar. He also made a short speech from one of the cars. We were all very impressed.

I was equally impressed with the chewing gum I got from American servicemen who took my Aunt Dorothy out. She took me along with her dates to dances at Purley and Croydon, where I'd watch them jitterbug; but I was more interested in the dance band.

In September 1944 the family returned south and I rejoined them. It was a very bleak time; food rationing was in force and the Perks family was very short of money. After school John and I went to the market in Maple Road to pick up damaged apples and vegetables thrown out by stall-keepers, taking them home to swell mother's meagre supplies. She sent us to the Cooperative bakery in Royston Road to buy stale loaves cheaply, and, while the man was getting it, we'd steal a fresh loaf. The stale loaf, soaked by Mum in water and then re-baked, came out as new, and we ate it with dripping, lard or sugar. If we had meat it was usually horsemeat or whale.

I was all the while becoming much more aware of girls, and we played kiss-chase on the bombed sites on the way home from school. I fell madly in love with Marjorie Baker, who lived behind us and was in my class. Sitting on the grass in Penge Recreation Park, she would comb my hair for hours. While all this romancing was going on for seven-year-old William Perks, Brussels was liberated, the battle of Arnhem took place and the first V2 rockets landed on England. Two months after I celebrated my eighth birthday, the famous bandleader Glenn Miller disappeared for ever while crossing the English Channel by plane.

At Christmas, big parties organised by Mum and Dad (who was home on leave) and Aunt Dorothy were attended by American servicemen and neighbours and there were sing-songs, with Dad on the piano. On these nights all the Perks brothers and sisters were packed into one bed, some at one end, some at the other, like a tin of sardines.

In April 1945, Mussolini was executed and Hitler shot himself in Berlin – but I was much more interested in a pretty, dark-haired girl, Jessie Brown. She lived in Anerley, but visited her grandmother who lived near us. I was madly in love with her and she knew it; she kept me hanging on a string for years.

On Tuesday 8 May, World War II ended in Europe. We celebrated with a wonderful street party and an enormous bonfire in the middle of the road. Whole staircases were burned, plus doors and beams from the bombed houses. Men were running up the stairs on one side, through the fire, and then down the stairs on the other side. It was a fabulous, exhilarating moment.

My second brother, Paul Edgar, was born on 2 June 1945 at Blenheim Road – obviously conceived nine months earlier on Mum's birthday, 2 September. Many years later I suddenly realised that John, Judy and I had all been conceived on Dad's birthday, 16 January.

I started going out regularly with Betty Southby, who lived in Arpley Road. Dating Betty was hazardous: her road was among the most dangerously violent in a vicious area: you didn't go down Arpley Road unless you really had to. Our street was tough enough, and some of the kids from it later ended up in reform school or prison. Local gangs from Blenheim Road would occasionally attack Arpley Road with bottles and stones, but astonishingly nobody was ever seriously hurt.

By now Mum and Dad were giving us each sixpence a week pocket-money, which we saved for our weekly treat at the Saturday-morning children's cinema at the Odeon or the Kings Hall. I was mesmerised by the cowboy serials (Tom Mix, Hopalong Cassidy, Roy Rogers and Bill Boyd), cartoons, and my favourite, Flash Gordon.

Upon returning to school in September, David Eastwood and I were so advanced that we were moved up an extra year in class and were asked to look after some of the backward pupils during lessons.

Mum and Dad seemed to be taking a lot more interest in us and taught us kids how to knit and embroider, and how to make rugs from canvas and old rags that we cut into thin strips.

On 24 October 1945, I celebrated my ninth birthday and on the 26th, Dad came home for twelve days' leave. As he had become skilful with a newly bought fretwork machine, he made me a wonderful fort for Christmas, one with castle battlements, a gate with a portcullis, a moat with mirrored glass for water and a drawbridge. The big disappointment was that he could not afford soldiers to accompany it. This was one of his very rare presents. Twenty-three years later, I scraped together enough to put down a deposit on an English manor house, Gedding Hall in Suffolk, which uncannily resembled that fort. And one of my hobbies became collecting military artefacts, including models of Scottish soldiers – probably a subconscious reaction to what I hadn't had as a child.

# TELLING YOUR OWN STORY

**10** **Many narratives are written to be told aloud. With a partner, think about the characteristics a told story should possess. Then plan, draft and write a short story which you and your partner could tell to children at a local primary school.**

- ☐ In this task, you are told from the start who the audience is for your writing but you will still need to think about the kind of shape and style your story will require. For example, how long should it be? Could it be set in your local area which will make it more familiar to the audience?
- ☐ Thinking about the focus for your story may make you consider your audience again. How will you be able to involve your listeners in the story?
- ☐ How will you organise and structure your story? Can you share the telling in some way by using more than one voice?
- ☐ What other features will your story need to have? To hold your audience's attention you may have to consider how to use a lot of description and direct speech as well as how to build your story gradually to an exciting ending.
- ☐ If you have the chance, try out your story on a younger group of children but not necessarily a whole class.

### *REWIND*

- Do not be afraid to experiment with narrative writing and do not expect all the narratives you read to have exactly the same form.
- When you are asked to write narrative, consider the possibility of changing the narrator or the narrative stance. Concentrate on writing for a particular reader. Before you plan and write, think of the effect you want your writing to have on him or her.
- Written narratives are some of the longest pieces of writing you will be asked to produce in school. Careful redrafting and revision as well as neat handwriting can make a difference in the effect they have on a reader.

# 8

# What it's worth

## COMPARISON AND ANALYSIS

One of the most important ways in which we use language to make sense of experience is by making choices. As you discuss with your friends what to do one Saturday evening, you add up the pros and cons of going to the cinema, meeting at a friend's house, staying in and watching television, doing extra homework or babysitting for a relative. The pros and cons are the arguments for or against doing a particular thing. Your decision – your choice – will probably be based on a number of factors, like whether you have any money, what the majority of your group want to do and what you yourself would most like to do. As you talk with your friends, these factors will keep coming into the conversation in one form or another but eventually you will find that – with a bit of compromise – most of you can agree on what to do.

If you tried to write an account of your discussion it would be hard to follow. The points made in favour of doing one thing rather than another would be spread out throughout the conversation, new choices would be suddenly introduced and people would very likely change their minds as the conversation progressed. Talk is like that. But if you want to come to the same kind of decision in writing, then you have to organise what you want to say more carefully.

UK & Ireland

# Tanked up in Taunton

EVEN in the driest summer you don't usually meet people walking down Taunton High Street carrying buckets of water on their heads, or bands of school children erecting emergency water tanks.

by Pat Simmons

But July 7-14 was "Oxfam in Taunton Week", and these were two of the activities designed to bring home to people what it's like to live far from clean water.

The week was the first in a series of special Oxfam appeals targeting individual towns. It's a brand-new approach by Oxfam to fundraising at a local level, a chance to speak more directly to existing supporters and reach out to new ones, especially young people.

Supporters and their friends learnt about the day-to-day work of a water engineer when Paul Sherlock, just back from Somalia, spoke at a special meeting. Fundraising events included concerts by the Bhundu Boys and George Melly and a collection following a recital by the Bristol First Bethel United Gospel Choir.

Water for Africa was the main focus of the week, which aimed to raise £25,000 for water projects in some of Africa's poorest communities. But, says Richard English, who co-ordinated the week from the Oxford end, people were the real target - people to become long-term Oxfam supporters, to help in the area's three Oxfam shops, or become members of the local Oxfam group.

Above all, Richard hopes that the week will give Taunton people a better understanding of the realities of lives of so many people in the Third World.

## Going, Going . . .

About 42 per cent of all tropical forest ha been removed over the past 500 years or s but most of this loss has occurred in the la 30 years. In the early 1980s forest areas in Africa were being cleared 29 times faster than they were being planted; in tropical America, this ratio was 10.5 to 1, and in tropical Asia 4.5 to 1. In the last ten years annual deforestation in the tropics has doubled to 20 million hectares.

Many countries have been rapidly denuded of valuable and productive forests Côte d'Ivoire, El Salvador, Haiti, Bangladesh peninsular Malaysia, Sri Lanka, Benin, Sierra Leone and Togo in the wetter tropics Many nations in the drier regions, especially the Sahel, have also been denuded of much of their dry woodlands.

Only 10 of today's 33 tropical-timber-exporting countries will have any timber left to export in the year 2000. In contrast, a very few countries still have the major part of their territory under forest. The following countries have extremely low population densities and – so far – lack the capability or economic opportunities to exploit the forests: French Guiana, Surinam, Guyana, Papua New Guinea and Zaire.

**1** **In your group, study the leaflet extracts on these pages. They are published by some of the groups which organise aid to majority world countries. Also look at these nine 'priorities' for aid agencies and, between you, try to decide on their order of importance by placing them in a diamond like the one shown here. Copying the keywords on to strips of paper which you can move around will help you to do this.**

| | | |
|---|---|---|
| **A** | SHELTER | Providing emergency tents and housing. |
| **B** | FOOD | Supplying enough food for everyone. |
| **C** | WATER | Providing enough water for the population and for farming. |
| **D** | IMMUNISATION | Inoculating children and adults against infectious diseases. |
| **E** | INFRASTRUCTURE | Building roads, schools and hospitals and encouraging new industry. |
| **F** | CONTRACEPTION | Giving free contraceptive advice to limit family size. |
| **G** | AGRICULTURE | Setting up projects to help people grow their own food. |
| **H** | MEDICINE | Providing drugs to combat diseases. |
| **I** | DEMOCRACY | Encouraging the development of democratic governments where all the people have a say in their own future. |

**most important**

**least important**

## Where the money goes...

...86 pence from every £1 spent goes on Save the Children's work overseas and in the UK.

- **65p** Work in Africa, Asia and rest of the world
- **21p** United Kingdom projects
- **11p** Publicity & fundraising
- **3p** General administration

- **Africa** £21,764,000
- **Asia** £10,900,000
- **Rest of the world** £5,521,000
- **United Kingdom** £12,178,000
- **Publicity & fundraising** £6,185,000
- **General administration** £1,810,000

For more information about Save the Children's work or a copy of the full Financial Accounts 1990/91, please write to: Save the Children, 17 Grove Lane, London SE5 8RD.

### IN FLIGHT AND IN FEAR

- Refugee numbers have almost doubled in the last 10 years.
- The money available to help them - money given by governments to the United Nations High Commissioner for Refugees (UNHCR) - has been halved in real terms.
- Displaced people - who are forced to move to another part of their country - are not counted in the official refugee figures and are not entitled to United Nations protection.
- Millions live in transit while hope fades. Many have lived for years in limbo in squalid camps.
- Children are at the sharp end of this suffering.

KURDISH REFUGEE FAMILY, ISIKVEREN CAMP, TURKEY / GISELLE DYE

## *Now write . . .*

As you have already learned, moving from talking to writing means that you have to think hard about exactly what you want to say and who you want to address. In doing this, you will be choosing to use a particular writing type. Using points from your discussion, you could go on to write your opinion about what you think the priorities should be for aid agencies in the future. Or you could write persuasively in order to encourage them to change their approaches. You would know about the need to think hard about the focus, purpose and audience for your writing as you did this.

## WAYS OF EVALUATING 1

Another way to write about these choices is to try to work out their importance and value in relation to one another – to compare them and contrast their features.

*Comparing and contrasting* a set of alternatives like these is a challenging writing task, making the most of your knowledge and drawing on all of your organisational skills. Sometimes in school, in Design and Technology, English or Geography, you will be asked to *evaluate* a number of proposals. Then, as well as comparing them, you will be expected to give your opinion about them and say which one you think is most suitable or appropriate. On other occasions you will be asked to *analyse* a problem or an issue and to define the arguments which lie behind it.

**2 The three writing tasks below ask you to compare, evaluate and analyse. With a partner, decide how you would set about writing each one. As you talk, think about:**

- the *focus* of the writing. Is the most important thing your (the writer's) views or the arguments which make up the subject?
- the *purpose* of the writing. Is it to inform, to explain, to persuade or to give an opinion? Or, is it a mixture of some or all of these?
- the *audience* for the writing. Is the writing for yourself, your friends, experts, or for anyone to read?

What does thinking about these questions imply for the way you should organise and structure your writing? Will you use the third person ('he', 'she', 'it') or the first ('I', 'we')? How will you group the information you include?

**A** Compare and contrast the short-term and long-term goals of aid relief agencies working in the majority world.

**B** Evaluate the aims of aid relief agencies in majority world countries.

**C** Analyse the range of problems which aid agencies face in assisting majority world countries.

3 Now look at some of the arguments for and against what is known as the 'continental' school day. More and more schools are opting to change to this pattern where school starts at 08:00, has a short break for lunch and finishes at 14:00 hours.

Here and on page 112 is a selection of views from a range of people. Read them carefully and make your own two lists of the arguments for and against the change. Put them in your own words.

| FOR | AGAINST |
|---|---|
| | |

**Sophie Harris – parent:** 'I don't like the idea of not knowing where the kids are every afternoon. They could be up to all kinds of mischief. And what if all the kids are going off to school at different times in the morning – it'll be like a shift system in our house.'

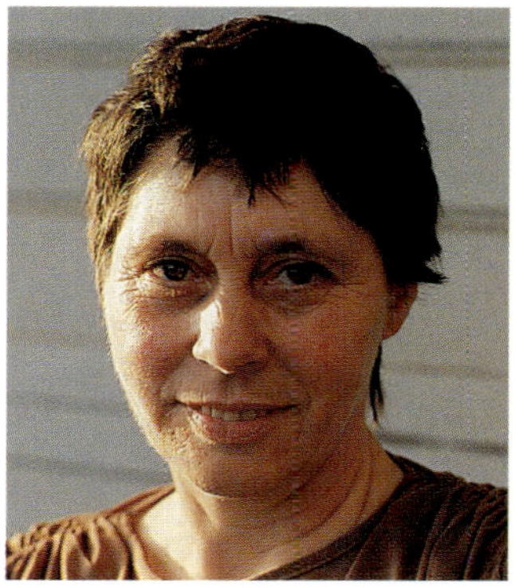

**Jane Turner – bus company manager:** 'This could throw out all our schedules. We have to get people to work in the mornings before the school rush starts.'

**Jeremy Bigley – Maths teacher:** 'The day will be a mad rush. We won't know if we're coming or going. Then, there'll be even more meetings after school!'

**Rachel – Year 12 pupil:** 'Those of us with part-time jobs at the supermarket might be able to increase our hours and get more money.'

**Kevin Richards – drama teacher:** 'That's goodbye to play rehearsals at lunchtimes. Will the cast really feel like staying on after school a couple of nights a week? I doubt it.'

**John Hanson – Deputy Head:** 'Lunchtimes are getting more and more difficult to supervise. The dinner ladies do their best but they can't really keep order.'

**Eric Gascoigne – school governor:** 'I like the idea of these children getting up early and working harder. That's what schools should be like.'

**Caroline Adams – Education Officer:** 'We could save on heating and possibly on maintenance costs and perhaps make money from letting the school facilities to other groups in the afternoon. And in winter students won't be going home in the dark.'

**Margaret Walsh – kitchen supervisor:** 'Me and my ladies are worried about our jobs. This'll just be another way to save money and forget about everything else. Don't forget that for lots of kids school-dinner is the main meal of the day.'

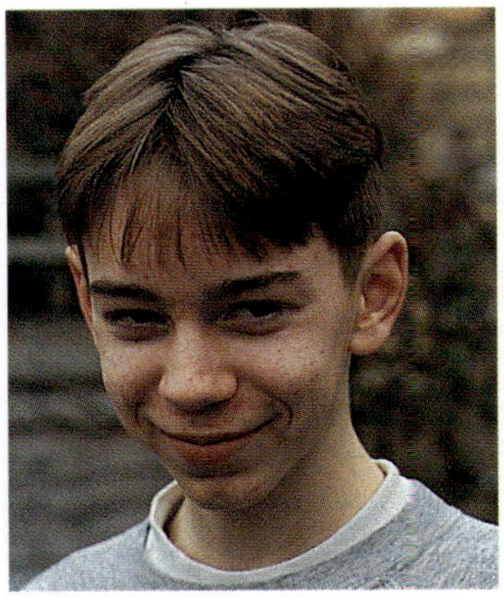

**Benny – Year 9 pupil:** 'There's nothing to do at lunchtime except play soccer and we have to go outside whatever the weather. Kids are always getting into trouble for things that happen at lunchtime.'

**Barbie Evans – Science teacher:** 'There's plenty of evidence that children concentrate better in the mornings and you always have to settle them down after a break. We could get more done with this new system.'

**Jaswinder Kandola – shopowner:** 'Lunchtimes are very busy. Often the kids from the school just wander round and get in the way of other customers and you have to keep a careful eye on one or two of them.'

**Sarah Knell – PE teacher:** 'I like having plenty of time for activities after school but if we're the only school that does it there'll be a lot of hanging about waiting to go to away fixtures or for visiting teams to arrive.'

**Gordon Sumner – parent:** 'It might seem like a good idea in summer when the mornings are bright but in winter, it can be dark until nearly nine o'clock – that's dangerous for children who cycle to school.'

**Ernie Crabtree – local resident:** 'At lunchtimes there are groups of kids wandering around the estate with nothing to do even when it's raining. They're nothing but a nuisance.'

**Alan Gates – curriculum co-ordinator:** 'Planning the timetable takes a lot of time and hours of meetings. We could start them at 2.30 and still be home by five o'clock.'

**4** **Review the lists you prepared for task 3. Which arguments are most important or most convincing? Which arguments directly contrast with one another? Rewrite the list matching arguments against one another.**

**5** **Now you are ready to write the first draft of your piece of writing. The title is:**

'Evaluate the arguments for and against the introduction of a continental day for schools for inclusion in a school magazine for parents.'

If the title was 'Consider the arguments . . .', 'Discuss the arguments . . .', or 'Compare and contrast the arguments . . .' you could probably approach your work in exactly the same way.

**To start with, write an opening paragraph which outlines what the writing is about.** It is clear that your audience, parents, will have some idea of the background to the subject. **Then, describe the arguments for and against.** There are two ways to do this. The simplest way would be to list all the positive arguments and follow them with all the negative ones. But, a better way might be to consider the *effects* of making the change and the good and bad consequences which could result. For example, cutting out the lunchtime break (the change) might lead to less disruption and trouble in the playground (an effect) but, on the other hand, there might be an increased risk of trouble as pupils make their way home in the afternoon (another effect). **Whichever way you choose to work, end your writing with a conclusion which gives your own views.**

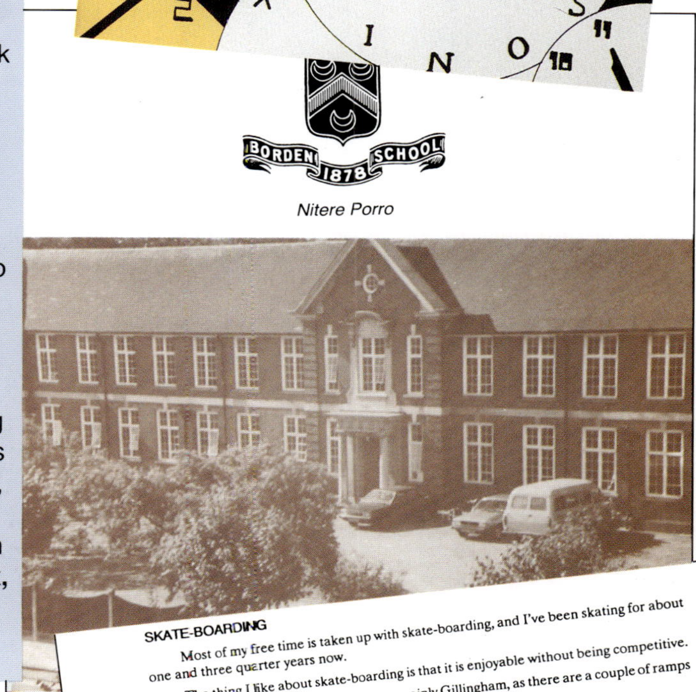

*Nitere Porro*

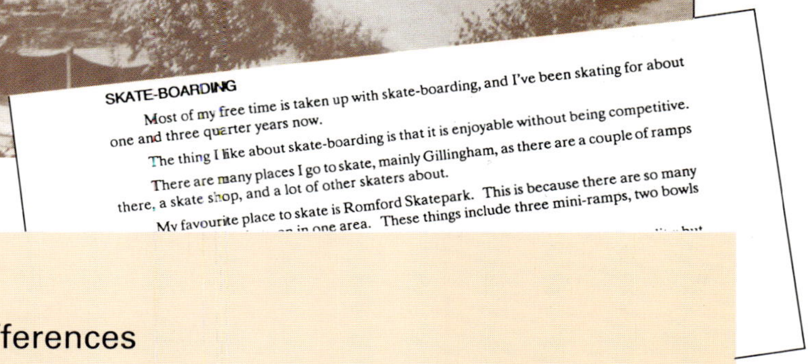
SKATE-BOARDING

Most of my free time is taken up with skate-boarding, and I've been skating for about one and three quarter years now.

The thing I like about skate-boarding is that it is enjoyable without being competitive.

There are many places I go to skate, mainly Gillingham, as there are a couple of ramps there, a skate shop, and a lot of other skaters about.

My favourite place to skate is Romford Skatepark. This is because there are so many ... in one area. These things include three mini-ramps, two bowls

**Words and phrases which compare:**

– by connecting ideas

and or but
on the other hand
although
instead
in contrast
alternatively

– by showing differences

| | |
|---|---|
| qualifiers: | better, very or more |
| comparatives: | small, smaller, smallest |
| opposites: | bigger/smaller |

*Redraft and final version*

**6** **Before you redraft, share your work with your partner or read your draft to a larger group. As you listen to other versions, note how other people have organised the arguments and expressed them in different ways. Think about which approaches are most effective and see how closely your writing matches the information given in factfile 11.**

**7** **Now correct and amend your first draft and, if you are happy with it, write your final version. If you have not already done so, you may need to use words and phrases to explain, like 'therefore' or 'because', and to link ideas, like 'in contrast' or 'on the other hand'.**

## FACTFILE 11 COMPARISON/ ANALYSIS

If you are asked to compare, evaluate or analyse, remember that:

- the *focus* of the writing is on the subject or subjects being compared
- the *purpose* of the writing is to examine the subject closely and, where there is more than one, to treat them equally
- the *audience* can be expected to have some understanding of the subject
- the writing should be objective and written largely in the third person
- each paragraph should develop a separate point or show a similarity or difference.

# LOOKING BACK – REVIEWING

In many school subjects, and particularly in Science and Technology, you will sometimes be asked to evaluate an experiment, a design or a sequence of work you have planned and tried out. After a geography field trip, for example, you could be asked to look back on the success of a survey or study. For all of these, you will need to look back on what you did and consider what you might have done differently or better and where you were most successful. You will be *reviewing* what happened.

A review starts as *informational writing*, includes your *opinion* and ends with an *evaluation*. In writing a review you need to draw on what you already know about the first two writing types. You can see that the *focus* of the writing changes as it develops. To begin with the subject and information connected with it is important, then the focus shifts to the writer's views. Finally, the evaluation shifts the focus back again to the subject.

THE WORD IS OUT

So 'The Word' is back for another series – a weekly hour's 'live fun' with Terry and our Amanda. This week we have a promised interview with Laura Dern, star of 'Wild at Heart'. This has to be the highlight of the show, I thought to myself.

But first we have Margie Clarke sitting on a sofa being offensive. Quick cut to a Stoke nightclub for more 'live fun', where three fat females are being paired off with three louts. Remember! Laura Dern interview later. Can't wait.

Back to the studio for some music from the 'Manic Street Preachers' who play some blurge for two minutes to an enthusiastic live audience roaming free round the set. Meanwhile Amanda De Cadenet wriggles her hips around the place. Little Terry reminds us once more of the exclusive Laura Dern interview coming up. I knew there had to be a reason I hadn't switched off.

We are now presented an insight into the rising popularity of American 'love game shows'. The girls tell us how much fluff 'he' has in his belly button and if 'he' picks his toenails. 'He' has to work out who said what about him. If 'he' guesses correctly they go on a date ... and this guy picks his toenails???

Only ten minutes left of the 'show' and still no Laura Dern. But it's back to Stoke .... cut back to Terry looking embarrassed once again ... introduce another live act ... chaos ... Margie Clarke being offensive again ..... roll credits.

No Laura Dern – no word – the word is out.

Alistair Graham

The evaluation on these pages was written by a GCSE student as part of his CDT coursework. See how the three stages – informational writing, opinion and evaluation – are identifiable in his writing.

EVALUATION OF FINAL STRUCTURE

Refer to photographs of finished model, and drawings (inc. force sheet.)

The evaluation consists basically of the following:

Wt to strength ratio

Units used (1 unit = 10 g)

Bridge cost.

Integrity / Weakness (analyse design fault, or construction fault, make criticisms, suggests methods whereby improvements might be made.

DEFLECTION.

Summary of construction.

The plan was basically met

The bridge was completed on time

The brief was satisfied by the finished project.

Aesthetically pleasing structure produced.

(1) STRENGTH TO WEIGHT RATIO

Firstly the weight of the bridge must be taken, using an electronic balance.

THE BRIDGE WEIGHT was 384·54g.

Since 1 unit of wood is given as 10g (for a piece of wood 10 × 10 × 200mm, (even though mine were cut to around 7 × 7 × 130)) my bridge is costed at

$\frac{384 \cdot 54}{10}$ units = 38·454 units.

Compared with others in my group, this bridge is quite light; it may possess more structural supports, but they are thinner in width, & shorter. However, the lightest bridge is not necessarily the weakest. With all the different weights, to analyse the best bridge (cost optimising) a strength to weight ratio must be obtained. To do this, the bridge is placed across a 600mm gap, and weights hung below the bridge. The following experiment shows fully how this was done.

TESTING THE BRIDGE

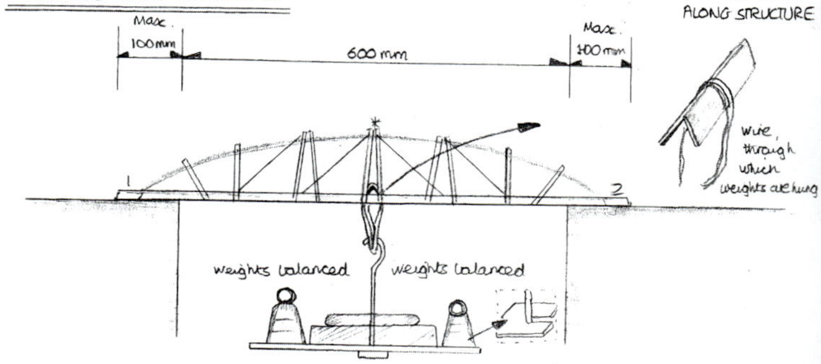


The metal bar (on which the wire was looped over and connected to the hook & weight table) was placed along the bottom, centre of the structure as shown. PLACING THE BAR ON THE TOP AT * WOULD NOT HELP MUCH MORE: (a) a bridge is generally subjected to weight on its bottom rails (eg: a road bridge) and it is hence more realistic to test the weights here.

(b) a specially designed weight table had been incorporated into the bridge. (see drawings).

(c) The bridge is so designed that any force applied to the bottom rail in turn tries to pull down / compress the upper laminated arch. But this is anchored at ends 1, 2, so won't compress easily unless they break. But points 1 & 2 are very strongly constructed specially to hold in the arch. (Hence, no movement of the bottom bar unless anchors 1 & 2 break and the upper bar pulls down. SEE JOINT SECTION NOTES & FINAL DRAWINGS & PHOTOS.

Then the weight table and hook (1kg approx) were looped onto the wire, and weights were gradually added. (A strain gauge could be used to help predict when the bridge is going to break NB: you can also hear it creaking when it's about to collapse.).

When the bridge breaks, the amount of mass needed to break it is noted down, and a strength : weight ratio then calculated.

C.GRIFFITH | 4B / 4X |

EVALUATION. | 0 | 16·11·90

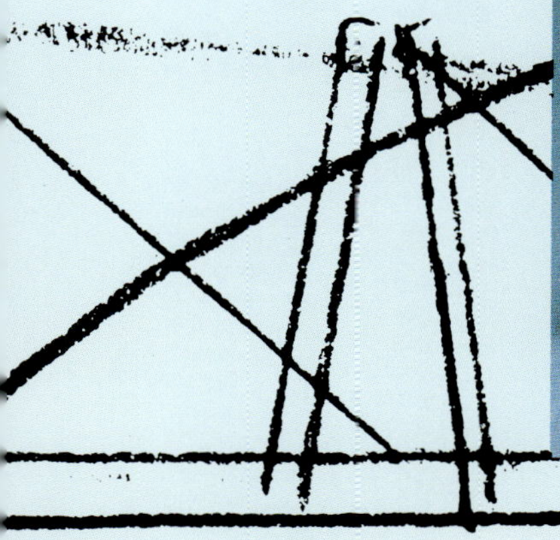

e bridge took 172·9 kg
thout breaking. A destruction-
eight couldn't be reached;
ith our limited amount of
masses. When 172·9 kg had
been loaded on the bridge, one
side of the bridge was bowing
slightly downwards at the bottom.
Deflection: about 3-4 mm. The
bottom rail must have been under
compression & tension to an extent.

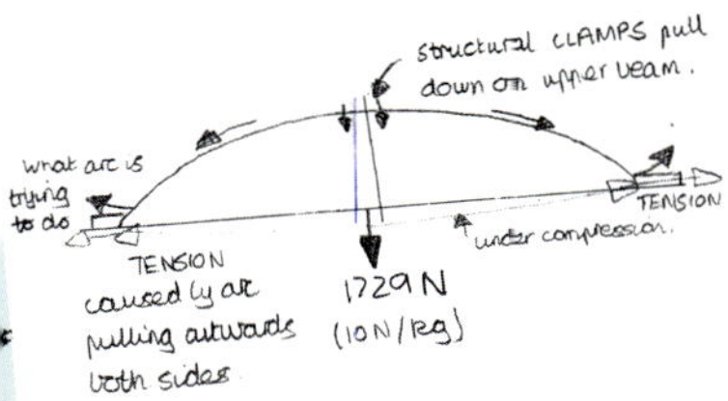


The STRENGTH : WEIGHT RATIO =

$$\frac{\text{MASS TAKEN (g)}}{\text{MASS OF BRIDGE}}$$

$$\Rightarrow \frac{173{,}000}{384{\cdot}54}$$

= 449·8

≃ 450 g : 1g

Mass taken : Mass of bridge.

C.GRIFFITH | 4B/4X |

So the strength : weight ratio
was approximately 450 to 1.
This is a sound ratio for a bridge.
Other ratios in my set ranged from
60:1 to about 350:1 (this part-
icular bridge took more weight than
mine, but was heavier. Overall, my
structure seemed well capable of
supporting a good amount of mass,
whilst itself being quite light.

Weakness. Final evaluation.

Since the bridge couldn't be taken
to breaking point, it is hard to
analyse any design faults, and
indeed through my research and
experiments the arch type design is
extremely good at handling loads.
However, several improvements could
have been

- ☐ better surface finishing of the product to reduce weight, and removal of redundant cross members (eg: across the top) which have no effect on strength, but if removed would aid the s/w ratio.
- ☐ Product was slightly wider than as required in the brief. Also, parts of vertical structures extend below the main span beam. This is against the rules of the project. However, bolsters placed under the ends of the bridge raise the the span level to offset this constr-uction feature, & placed correctly, decrease the width effective on the supporting banks.

- ☐ The structure is slightly distorted when viewed end on after assembly, due to differences of the relative shapes of the laminated (arc) sections. Improvement could have been made here: more accurate former and clamping method; ; method whereby two sides are spanned together, and joined; and cutting and finishing

Critism of written work
More research needed; better media studies, library research.

Better planning required. Also, more models might be implemented.

Future work?
Another bridge could be built taking the above notes into account, perhaps with different materials.

Work and research looking at tension limits of wood under force.

Research into other bridges (eg: cantilever, suspension) where different properties and forms of structure are involved

1·90

**8** **Look back on some of your own work in Science or Technology and select one experiment or design task. Write a review of what you did, saying what you tried to do, what went well and how you might have approached your task in different ways.**

## MEDIA REVIEW

A book, television, film or record review works in a similar way by looking at how successful the writers, programme makers, actors and directors or performers have been. Here, instead of saying what you did, you will need to describe what happens or what the book, programme, film or record is like and then give your comments on how you enjoyed it, what you found interesting about it and how successful it is likely to be.

### DIRE STRAITS

**On Every Street**
VERTIGO 510160

After a six-year silence, generally negative critical reaction smacked more of attitudes struck than a record accorded due consideration. Utterly free of the comingback star's usual overstressed-ego problems, the dozen songs probably amount to Dire Straits' best album. Restoring the tight editorial control from Sultans Of Swing days, Knopfler's writing packs in any amount of pungent humour (Heavy Fuel, My Parties), dark drama (Fade To Black, You And Your Friend) and more easy philosophising (The Bug, How Long). Musically, it kicks down no doors, but through sheer coherence of word and note hard-won in every beat, On Every Street simply satisfies.

# BEAR UP, BISON

**BUFFALO TOM/ SEX POD**

TT THE BEARS, BOSTON.

**ROCK 'N' ROLL is too ordinary a term to describe Buffalo Tom's arousal of suspense, curiosity and desire. So God gave rock'n'roll to you. And what else did you get? You got rock'n'roll parodying itself. Kiss, Skid Row, Guns N' Roses. They go through the same old routine: Make a pretend gut-wrench of a hilariously bad record, please the deskbound with their "bad boy" antics, hope to die before they get old, but, well, (their) life just manages to be a little too good for that, doesn't it? All this wrings the blood, emotion and mystery out of rock'n'roll. Buffalo Tom, who claim nothing more than to be three regular kinda guys, play music that makes your own throat threaten to seize up and choke you to death.**

**Before they get to amble on to the wee TT The Bears stage, there's this band called Sex Pod playing. Great name. Karen, the singer and guitarist used to be in Gut Bank. Wow! She's got this Edie Brickell-ish way of sounding laid-back but sort of overcome by violent feelings at the same time. The really rather post-college audience is astonished by this strange little unit of two girls who wouldn't look out of place in a nanny's agency and the jock on drums. Sex Pod are totally mag… Buffalo Tom have t…**

CINEMA RELEASE **HOT SHOTS (12)**

Directed by Jim Abrahams, starring Charlie Sheen, Lloyd Bridges, Valeria Golino.

Nowhere near as funny as Airplane! but light years ahead of the diabolical Repossessed, this latest in the current wave of movie satires hits only some of its targets as it takes pot-shots at various cinematic sitting ducks. Called out of youthful retirement to lead a critical air raid, square-jawed squadron leader Topper Harley (Sheen) dons the Top Gun shades and takes to the skies. Much face-slapping, bum-kicking jollity ensues as he romps through a succession of sight gags, aided and abetted by granite-faced straight man Lloyd Bridges, in fine form as a reconstructed war veteran with a few spare parts missing. Top moments include a reprise of the dreadful "sexy food" sequence from Nine And A Half Weeks in which Charlie Sheen cooks a full English breakfast on his lover's sizzling stomach; other less laughable interludes find writers Abrahams and Proft taking obscure swipes at Diner with baffling results. Inconsistent then, but boosted by intermittent bouts of hilarity. And not a single farting joke in sight. ★★★

*Mark Kermode*

Television

## Morse is sidelined in game of murder

**CRITIC'S CHOICE**

★ **Inspector Morse – Happy Families**
ITV: 8.00 - 10.00 pm
With a psychotic murderer bent on bumping off members of a feuding aristocratic business dynasty one by one in the imposing setting of a mansion complete with drawbridge and castellated walls, I couldn't help but expect Miss Marple to pop up at any minute. Indeed, the opening hour of this week's episode has John Thaw smiling knowingly and camping it up for all he can.

As Morse makes his initial visit to the Balcombe ancestral heap, he asks Detective Sergeant Lewis: "Is there a butler?" "No sir," replies Lewis. "Pity. Might have saved a lot of time."

Morse is at a loss to make rhyme or reason of this case, hindered by an ambitious Chief Superintendent Holdsby (masterfully played by Alun Armstrong) who sees the quick solution of the murder as the ideal opportunity to further his career. And why is there no sense of grief emanating from the Balcombe's?

Anna Massey plays the mentally deranged Lady Balcombe, mother of two quite ghastly childish adult sons. As a seedy, bitter, failed Oxford student turned tabloid journalist, Rupert Graves jabs another sword into poor old Morse's side, making him the front page focus of press attention.

As each murder occurs it becomes apparent that someone is hellbent on revenge. For what? Morse can only stand by the sidelines and watch life and death unfold before him.

**DS**

Books

■ **The Book of the Banshee**
by Anne Fine (Hamish Hamilton £8.99). Furious adolescent Estelle wears grotty 'aubergine' makeup and might as well be an aubergine herself when it comes to responding to discipline. Her brother comically likens the family scene to William Saffery's account of the First World War. Enjoyable, amusing and craftily plotted, though it seems likely that parents may be more appreciative of its subject than teenagers.

### CURRICULUM GUIDES

**Curriculum Confidential Two.** By Jim Sweetman. Bracken Press, Newton Regis, Tamworth, B79 0NH. £5.60. 1 874254 00 1.

Updated since September 1991, each of the subject sections now summarises the programmes of study, lists the attainment targets and describes the major strands within them. Curriculum Confidential Three will be published next September.

**9** **With a partner look closely at the reviews on these pages. They are taken from newspapers and magazines. Consider what they have in common. Try to identify points in the writing where:**

- ☐ the focus is clearly on the subject
- ☐ information is objectively presented
- ☐ the third person is used.

**Also, think about the audience for these reviews. What can you tell about the readership of the magazines by the way in which the reviews are written and the kinds of information and opinion they present?**

Videos

● **Video choice**

**Barry Norman,** *writer and presenter, Film '91*
The better the film, the less it will work on video, but it's better to see a film on video than not at all. Cyrano de Bergerac *(Artificial Eye)* is as good a film as there is. It's extraordinarily well made and Gerard Depardieu is one of the best movie actors in the world. His performance is remarkable.

**10** **Write your own reviews of two of the following for inclusion in a magazine for teenagers:**

— a book you have recently read and enjoyed
— a current television series you watch
— a film or video you have recently seen.

**Make sure that you do not merely give an account of events. Be careful to make points, to write objectively and to use paragraphing.**

Review

**11** The best-selling game Trivial Pursuit costs £39.99 at Hamleys. The same game costs £26.87 at Toys R Us.

*REWIND*

- As you compare make sure that you treat both aspects equally and make each paragraph contain a single difference.
- When you evaluate, blend your views with your analysis of the subject.
- As you review, be careful not to write an account of what you did, read or watched.

# 9

# Writing in progress

## *PROJECTS, TOPICS AND THEMES*

You may well be asked to write some form of longer, or extended, writing such as a project, work on a particular topic or theme, or a field study as part of your GCSE courses. Later, in further education or at work, the kind of writing tasks you encounter may well be of the same sort. You could be asked to write a detailed report, an analysis of a particular problem or an evaluation of a new machine or process.

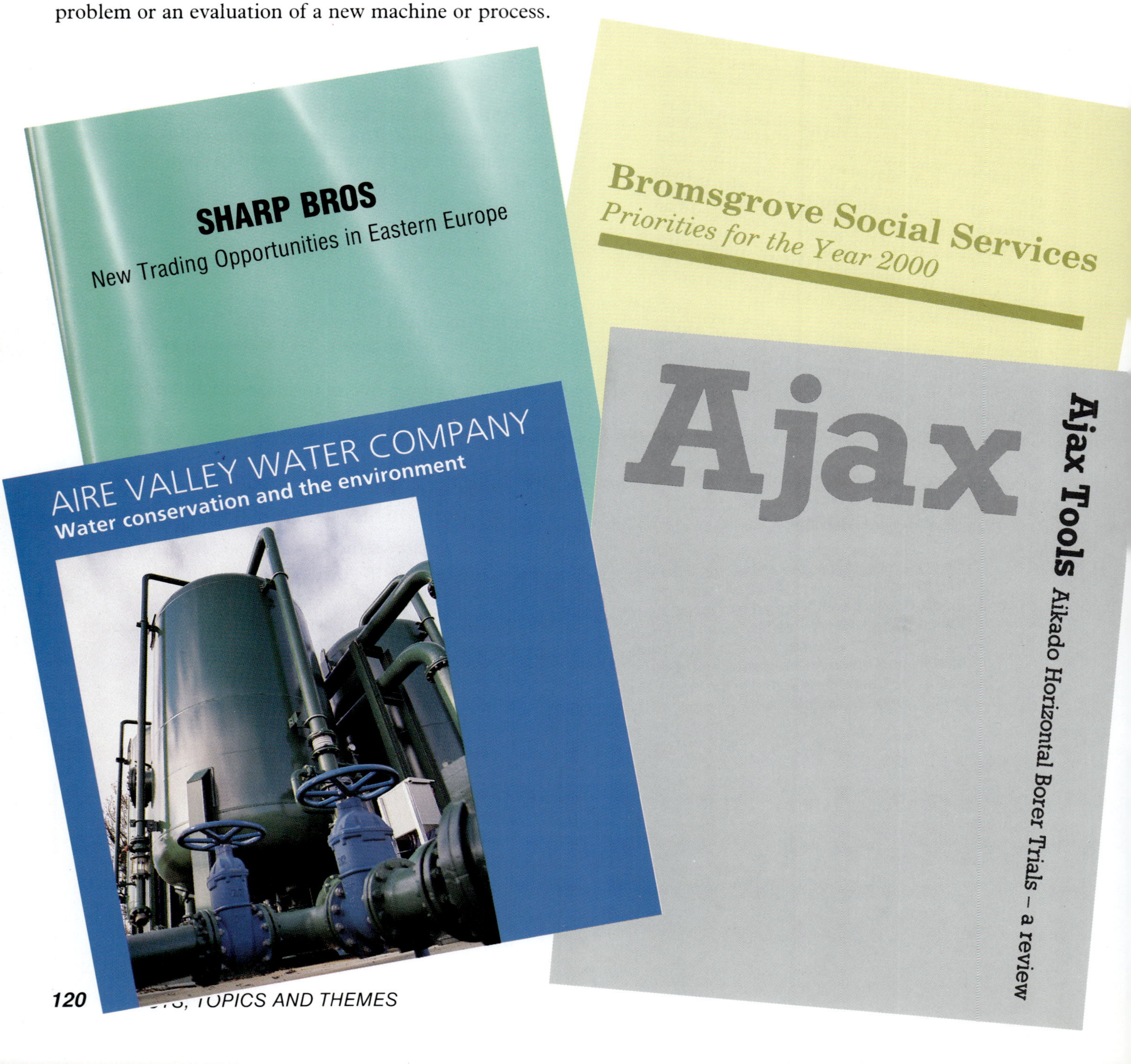

# ANALYSE YOUR TASK 1

When you are faced with a lengthy task of this kind, the first challenge is to decide exactly what you are being asked to do. It can be helpful to break down the task into a number of sections and then to see what different types of writing you will need to make use of.

**1 Imagine that you and a partner work for Sodaworks, a company which produces canned soft drinks. The company are keen to expand into Europe and to sell their drinks in a new market. They have identified Sweden as a country where the major companies do not yet have a foothold. They have sent you both on a week's visit to investigate the possibilities of a link with a Swedish company, Myrond, and to report back. On pages 122–124 is your diary of the trip.**

- ☐ Your company requires a full report on the trip written by the pair of you but, in the short term, your managing director wants a brief memo which she can present to a board meeting tomorrow. Think hard about this task. You know who your audience is but what should the focus for your writing be? Should it be to inform? Or to persuade? Will you write in the first person ('I') or write more objectively using the third person? How will you organise your writing? In what order will you present it? Should you aim for a chronological account (the order in which events took place) or group the information in another way?
- ☐ With your partner, decide on the five most important things you have to say to the Board (your audience). Then decide on the focus for your writing, the person you will use and the way you will organise the writing.

  **Write a first draft of your memo.**
- ☐ Exchange your draft with your partner and *analyse* each other's writing. Using the same headings of focus and organisation, see how your partner has set out to structure their writing and where they have been successful.

**MONDAY:** Arrived at Gatwick by 09:30 in plenty of time with no hold-ups on the M25 for a change. Plane delayed, so we had time for a leisurely breakfast. My partner, Sue, tells me that the Coca Cola company are lookng for new top management and she is thinking of applying. Flight was fine and we made up some of the lost time. Carl Sondstrom (Myrond's Deputy Chief Executive) met us at the airport and took us straight to their distribution plant which is 8 kilometres outside Stockholm. It's set in quite flat, attractive countryside on a new industrial estate with some additional building taking place at the moment. The railway runs close by, as does one of the country's motorways. Lunch with the Managing Director, Jon Bogenberg. Over some pleasant smorgasbord, he indicated that Myrond was also looking to expand their distribution activities. They already handle a wide range of soft drinks but our Freshkool Orange, Bilberry and Raspberry Yogurt flavours would go down well. He gave us copies of their latest company report (financial year ending last December) and some of their promotional material. They seem to have expanded considerably in the past few years as larger supermarkets have been developed throughout the country. Later in the afternoon, we toured the warehouse. There is some capacity there so they could store our products without any problem. Then back to Stockholm and our hotel with Carl. We were both very tired so had an early night.

**TUESDAY:** Carl picked us up at 09:00. This morning we visited two supermarkets and in the afternoon had a presentation about the way the distribution network operates. I found this a bit hard to follow but the gist is that they operate very much as we do in the UK but are equipped to be more diverse. It struck me that perhaps we could be handling a small range of other products with the same kind of outlets as we have. All the distribution operation is computer-controlled - orders, warehousing and even the routing of the products is co-ordinated which must save some time and energy.

In the evening, back to the hotel. Sue and I went out for dinner in a really pleasant floating restaurant on one of the lakes near the city. Excellent food but a bit hard on the expenses account! I haven't really talked that much to Sue Harrington before and we had a nice time. I told her about my problems with Sharon last year and apparently she has had this longstanding thing which broke up last year. We talked for ages and it was almost two o'clock by the time I got into bed.

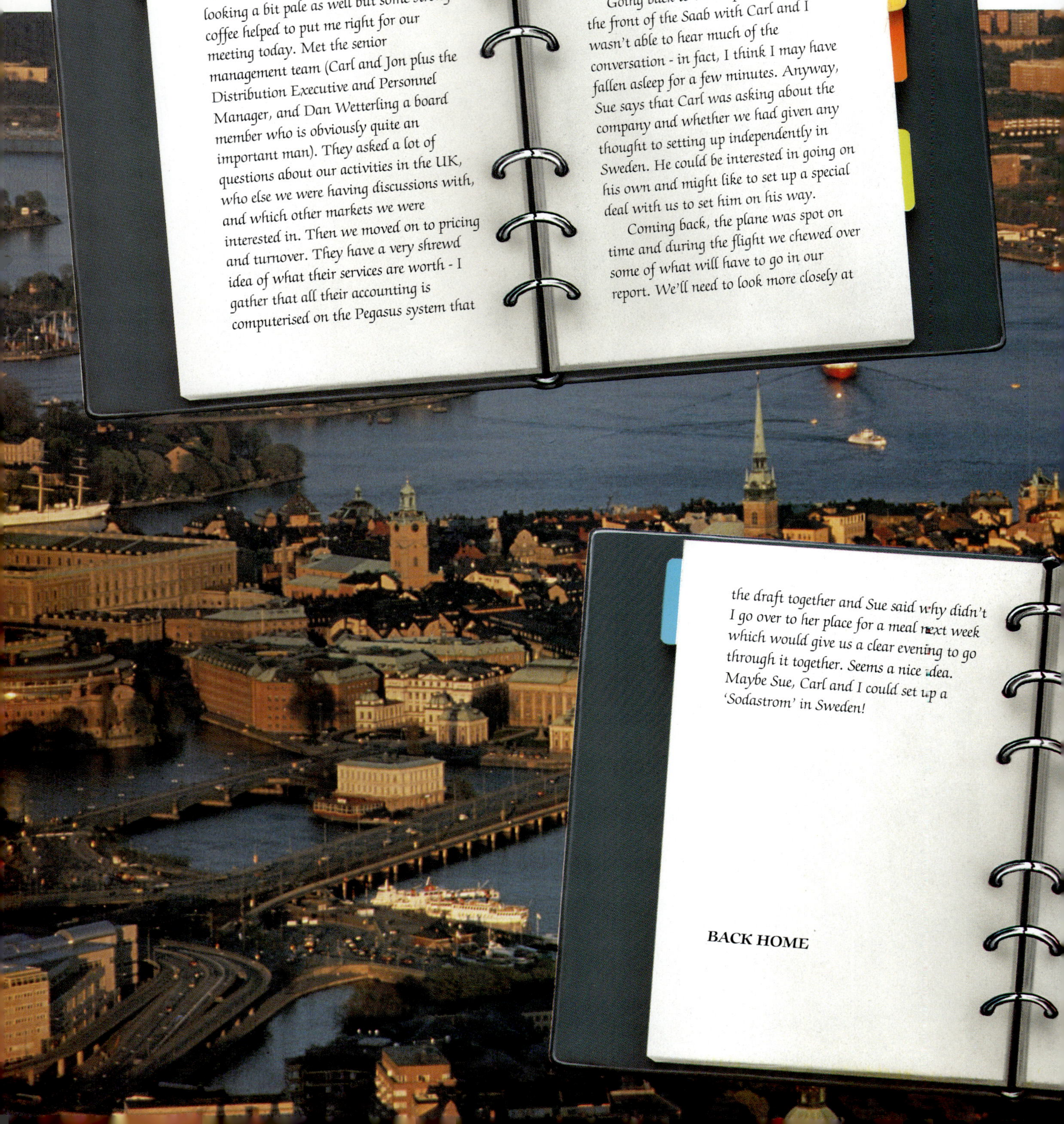

**WEDNESDAY:** Rather a painful head this morning. The Swedish vodka slips down very pleasantly but I think maybe I had a little too much last night. Sue was looking a bit pale as well but some strong coffee helped to put me right for our meeting today. Met the senior management team (Carl and Jon plus the Distribution Executive and Personnel Manager, and Dan Wetterling a board member who is obviously quite an important man). They asked a lot of questions about our activities in the UK, who else we were having discussions with, and which other markets we were interested in. Then we moved on to pricing and turnover. They have a very shrewd idea of what their services are worth - I gather that all their accounting is computerised on the Pegasus system that we use which could be helpful. Nothing too specific was said but they are clearly interested. They asked for top-level discussions as the next stage in sealing up a deal.

Going back to the airport, Sue sat in the front of the Saab with Carl and I wasn't able to hear much of the conversation - in fact, I think I may have fallen asleep for a few minutes. Anyway, Sue says that Carl was asking about the company and whether we had given any thought to setting up independently in Sweden. He could be interested in going on his own and might like to set up a special deal with us to set him on his way.

Coming back, the plane was spot on time and during the flight we chewed over some of what will have to go in our report. We'll need to look more closely at the draft together and Sue said why didn't I go over to her place for a meal next week which would give us a clear evening to go through it together. Seems a nice idea. Maybe Sue, Carl and I could set up a 'Sodastrom' in Sweden!

**BACK HOME**

**2** **Now think about the longer report. Look back at the diary (pages 122–124) and decide on:**

- ☐ three pieces of information you would leave out of a report;
- ☐ anything you might mention to your own managing director in confidence to help her deal with the company in the future.

**Below is a list of possible section headings for your report. Decide on the four or five of these you would think are most important and the order in which you would include them.**

**A** A brief history of Sweden and the company

**B** Company accounts for 1991–92

**C** The company structure

**D** Existing distribution network in Scandinavia

**E** Senior personnel

**F** An account of the trip to Sweden

**G** Comparison of their and our existing distribution networks

**H** Opportunities to work together in the future

**I** Current product stocklist

Compare your decisions with those made by others in the group.

# ANALYSE YOUR TASK 2

**3** **Below are a number of longer tasks which might be set in a variety of school subjects. For each one, make notes on the types of writing you might need to make use of.**

**Music:** As part of your music course you have visited a recording studio for the day and watched a rap singer and backing group make their first recording together. Think of four pieces of writing that you could produce after your visit.

**Art:** You have been asked to examine and give your own views about the ways that women are presented in paintings from a particular period of history. Which writing types do you think you might have to use in doing this?

**English:** After reading two novels by Thomas Hardy you have been on a study weekend to Dorset where Hardy lived and wrote his novels. As part of the weekend you visited the ancient stone circle at Stonehenge. Invent three tasks which expect you to compare, to reflect or describe, and to evaluate.

**Geography:** After a field trip to a National Park, where you conducted a survey and made some land use maps, you have been asked to explore the conflicting demands placed on such areas by farming, forestry, military use, reservoirs and recreation. Think of a way to plan your writing in three sections, each using a different writing type.

**Science:** As a piece of individual research you have looked into different accounts from a range of cultures and times which explain the origins of the universe. You now have to write these up into a single report with four or five sections. What writing types might you use?

**History:** Your class group has worked together on the changing roles of women in society since Victorian times. Think of five different ways you could follow up your research in writing using different writing types.

**Technology:** Your class has been working on the design of a new aid that elderly people will be able to use. Each of you has been asked to evaluate someone else's design. What types of writing might you make use of in your evaluation?

## WRITING YOUR RESPONSE

You have seen that the first stage in working on an extended task is to think hard about it and to analyse exactly what it requires you to do. As you go on to plan and draft your writing, keep the particular writing type you are aiming for in your mind as you work. Follow this plan for success:

| | |
|---|---|
| 1 | Study your topic task or your subject area carefully and decide on the different writing types you will have to use to be successful in your writing. The choice of these will depend largely on the task you have been set, or have set yourself. |
| 2 | Once you have decided on a writing type for a section of the writing, keep it clearly in your mind as you start to plan. Think hard about the ordering of your sections and, if necessary, your audience. For example, how detailed an introduction will you need to provide background information for your audience? Where will sketch maps, charts and tables help to make your writing clearer? |
| 3 | Once you have planned and are ready to start drafting your work, think about the characteristics of the writing type you have chosen alongside the content of your writing. Make sure you are confident about your purpose in a particular section and that you know what the main focus of your writing should be. Think about the organisation of your material and the language features your writing is likely to reveal. |
| 4 | As you check your first draft, think about the type of writing you are using as much as the content and presentation of your work when you re-read. Make sure that your choice of a writing type is sustained throughout a section. Make sure that where you explain you have not started to give an account, that where you compare you have done more than describe, and that where you persuade you have done more than just give your opinion. This kind of careful re-reading can be most important. |
| 5 | Before you write your final draft, check that each section links to the following one; that your introduction and conclusion are detailed enough and that your spelling of technical words from the subject you are discussing is secure. Use sub-headings where they will contribute to the overall effectiveness of your writing and, if necessary, include a bibliography at the end of your writing with a list of the books and sources you have used. |

**4** **Select a task from those given on page 126 or from your current work in other subject areas. Accompany the final draft with your own commentary, setting out what you were trying to achieve in your writing and evaluating how far you feel you have been successful.**

### REWIND

- Remember that longer tasks are made up of shorter sections, each of which make their own demands on you as a writer.
- Analysing writing tasks before you begin to write is the way to help each section of the writing achieve its purpose.
- As the writing goes on, check back and make sure that the features of the writing type are appearing in your writing. Asking a friend or your teacher to read your drafts through can help with this.

## RULES FOR 'ROOT THE LOOT' (pages 84–85)

INSTRUCTIONS

A game for two players.
One commands three moles on a midnight raid while the other controls three ferrets who are guarding the loot.

**Moles**

Your objective is to pick up as much loot as possible and return it to the safety of HQ without being caught by the ferrets. Each time you land in a tent section, shout 'Root the Loot', then add the loot score to the running total for that mole. You may return to the same loot as often as you like before returning to HQ. Be sure to conceal your running totals from the ferrets. Remember you are specially trained kamikazi raiders and will do anything, even sacrifice yourself and your loot, to help a comrade with a higher running total escape the ferrets and get back to HQ. The final raid score is your only concern.

**Ferrets**

Your objective is to capture all the moles as quickly as possible before too much is lost. To capture a mole, simply land on the same space, either on the surface or underground. The mole then forfeits any score he or she is carrying and is removed from the board.

MOVES

Moves on the surface are from one tent section to another or to and from adjacent guy rope areas. Underground, one move is from one tunnel junction to another. Moles are faster than ferrets and must always move two spaces. This can include one space forward and one space back if desired. As long as one mole turn follows one ferret turn, any one of the opposing teams may make a move. One mole may be out rooting whilst two wait in HQ for a good opportunity to emerge. Similarly, ferrets may find it advantageous as a team to have two on guard whilst one chases. Ferrets may never enter the moles' HQ.

YOU WILL NEED

Three ferret counters, three mole counters, paper and pencil. Mark each mole counter A, B and C so it is clear when keeping running totals which mole is carrying what score.

TO BEGIN

Place one ferret in any section of each tent and the moles anywhere in HQ. Moles can then begin their raid. The first raid ends when all moles have been captured. When all moles have been lost make a grand total of their safe loot scores and enter it on the Grand Score Card under Raid One. Players then swap roles. The ferret player takes over the moles to play Raid Two and tries to beat the Raid One score to win.

# Credits

The model of genre developed in **Language Links 2** owes a debt to the work of the LINC (Language in the National Curriculum) Project 1991 and the writings of David Crystal. The use of the term 'focus' is derived from the author's work with the SAIL Literary Scheme and the research conducted by Tom Christie and Pam Owen at Manchester University which led to its establishment. Special thanks to Jessica Rood.

The school magazine on page 113 (T), the Technology evaluation on pages 116-17 and the photographs on pages 115 (C) and 116-17 are reproduced by kind permission of Colin Griffith and the staff of Wilson's School, Wallington, Surrey. The Science report on page 29 is reproduced by kind permission of Anna Putnis; and for the review on page 115 we thank the author Alistair Graham and John Sutton, Head of English at Netherhall School, Cambridge. The Geography trip report on page 115 and the article/school magazine on page 113 (B) are reproduced by kind permission of the staff and pupils of Borden Grammar School, Sittingbourne.

The tasks on pages 77 and 78 are adapted from those set for the MEG GCSE English examination in 1990. We thank MEG for permission to reproduce these.

The author and editor would also like to thank all the people who helped with the handwritten extracts in this book.

**ILLUSTRATORS**

Christie Archer 46-7, 56, 63, 86, 108-9, 118-19,
Philip Bannister 30-1
Evelyn Bartlett 22, 74-6,94-5
Paul Bateman 78
Jane Bennett 88
John Boult 16
Peter Clark 51
Peter Dennis 35
Linda Garland 24-5
Stuart Hughes 20, 26-7, 32, 44, 46-7, 49, 50, 59, 72-3, 82, 88, 98, 120-3
Jane Human 92-3
Tony Kerins 98-100
Sue Lines 13, 14, 103-5
Fiona McVicar 64-5
ML Design 17, 21, 43, 73, 115
David Mostyn 18-19
Simon Mulligan 16
Andrea Norton 52-4
Peter Owen 114
Peter Tucker 15
Sharon Pallent 89-91
Viv Quillin 12
Karen Tushingham 102